U1001541

浙江省社会科学界联合会社科普及课题成果
浙江金融职业学院国际贸易实务国家高水平专业群建设项目阶段性研究成果

寻找浙里的乡愁印记

——浙江古村落文化寻踪

王慧盛 编著

浙江工商大学出版社
ZHEJIANG GONGSHANG UNIVERSITY PRESS
·杭州·

1月 January

鱼文化节
Fish Culture Festival

文化寻踪之推荐日历
Recommended Month

鱼文化节

Fish Culture Festival

文化寻踪之浙里村落 Ancient Villages

➢ 南浔区和孚镇荻港村

Digang Village, Hefu Town, Nanxun District

荻港村，地处杭嘉湖平原，是一个具有1300多年历史的水乡古村落。四面环水，河港纵横；青堂瓦舍，临河而建的荻港自古就有“苕溪渔隐”之称，拥有南苕胜境、总管堂、演教禅寺、礼耕堂等景点。这里到处都是“小桥、流水、人家”的意境和“民和、家兴、业旺”的繁荣。在荻港，除别处可看到的老街古宅、亭台楼阁外，还可以体会那种久违的、逝去的但仍怀念着的水乡生活。

Digang Village, located in the Hangzhou-Jiaxing-Huzhou Plain, is an ancient water village with a history of over 1,300 years. Featuring netted rivers and stained quaint buildings, Digang has been known as “Tiaoxi

Fishing and Seclusion Village" since ancient times, which depicts the ideal quiet and tranquil lifestyle near the Tiaoxi River. It boasts many scenic spots such as Nantiao Attraction, General Administration Hall, Yanjiao Temple, and Ligeng Hall. Visitors will be immersed in the peaceful scene of "small bridges and families aside flowing rivers" and the prosperity of "harmonious community and hard-working families". In Digang, in addition to the old houses, pavilions that can be seen elsewhere, visitors can also experience the passing, long-lost, but still nostalgic life in the water town.

文化寻踪之浙里印记 Cultural Imprints

建筑文化
Architectural Culture

南苕胜境 Nantiao Attraction

南苕胜境是一处道家的胜地，位于荻港古镇的东南隅。其建于元代，后毁于兵火，成于"乾嘉盛世"。当时是一座建筑群，其中以云怡堂、积川书塾最为有名。云怡堂建于乾隆三十四年（1769），分前后两进，前为文昌阁，后为纯阳楼，供吕纯阳祖师。积川书塾原为荻港章氏私家书塾。清朝200多年间，积川书塾出了50多位进士，以及100多名太学生、贡生、举人，在历史上曾名噪一时。

Nantiao Attraction, located in the southeast of Digang Town, has been a Taoist resort. The site, built in the Yuan Dynasty, was later destroyed in the war, and was known to the world until the years of "Emperor Qianlong and Jiaqing Heyday" (in the Qing Dynasty). Back then, the site was a building complex, among which Yunyi Hall and Jichuan School were the most famous buildings. Built in the 34th year of Emperor Qianlong's reign (1769), Yunyi Hall was divided into two rows of constructions. The front one called Wenchang Pavilion, while the back one called Chunyang Tower. Chunyang Tower was dedicated to Lv Chunyang, the Taoist immortal. Jichuan School used to be the old-style private school of a Zhang family in Digang. Throughout the more than 200 years of the Qing Dynasty, Jichuan School cultivated more than 150 top scholars of the nation, which enjoyed quite a reputation in history.

演教禅寺 Yanjiao Temple

演教禅寺,始建于唐后周显德二年(955),距今已有千余年历史,经明清多次扩建占地已达二十余亩。步入演教禅寺的大门,青石镌成的石弥陀迎面而坐,笑口常开,栩栩如生。寺内古柏成荫,清净异常,铜钟传音,声波四溢,数里之外,还清晰可闻。寺内大雄宝殿顶悬钢镜,上有"国泰民安,风调雨顺",系明丞相严嵩所题,其内设的诸多神像无论形态太小,均可与杭州灵隐寺媲美。演教禅寺是自宋朝以来,湖州城南的佛教中心。

Built in the second year of the reign of Emperor Xiande in the Later Zhou Dynasty (955), Yanjiao Temple has a history of more than a thousand years, covering an area of more than 13,333m^2 after expansion in the Ming and Qing Dynasties. In front of the gate sit the stone Amitabha Buddha vividly smiling, which are rare among Huzhou's temples. In the temple, the old cypresses are shaded, clean and unusual, and the bronze bells transmit clear sound which is audible a few miles away. A steel mirror hangs on the top of the Grand Hall, on which there's an inscription written by Yan Song who was the councellor-in-chief of the Ming Dynasty, reads, "Guo Tai Min An, Feng Tiao Yu Shun" (The country prospers and the people enjoy peace. The wind and rain come in their time.). The statues of Buddha are so exquisite and lifelike. They compare favourably with those in Hangzhou Lingyin Temple. Yanjiao Temple has been the Buddhism center in the south of Huzhou City since the Song Dynasty.

➢ 名人文化 Celebrity Culture

章荣初 Zhang Rongchu

章荣初（1901—1972），原名吉初，又名增华，祖籍浙江湖州荻港，因他父亲章清儒在菱湖经营同丰祥丝庄而迁居菱湖。章荣初毕生致力实业，为家乡的经济、文化建设做出了巨大贡献。

Zhang Rongchu (1901-1972), formerly known as Jichu, also known as Zenghua, was born in Digang, Huzhou, Zhejiang. He moved to Linghu because his father Zhang Qingru ran Tongfengxiang Silk Store there. He devoted his life to develop enterprises. He made great contributions to the economic and cultural construction of his hometown.

章鸿钊 Zhang Hongzhao

章鸿钊（1877—1951），生于浙江吴兴县（今浙江省湖州市），地质学家、地质教育家、地质科学史专家，中国科学史事业的开拓者。章鸿钊创办了农商部地质研究所（地质讲习班），为我国培育了第一批地质学家，其中许多人成为我国早期地质工作的主力。他从近代地质科学角度研究了中国古籍中有关古生物、矿物、岩石和地质矿产等方面的知识，开创我国地质科学史研究之先河，具有深远影响，为我国地质界的一代宗师。

Zhang Hongzhao (1877–1951), born inWuxing County, Zhejiang Province (today's Huzhou City), was a geologist, a geological educator, an expert in the history of geological science, and a pioneer in the history of Chinese science. He founded the Institute of Geology (Geological Workshop) of the Ministry of Agriculture and Commerce, and cultivated the first batch of geologists for the country. Many of them later became the main force in the early geological work. He studied the knowledge of paleontology, minerals, rocks and geological minerals in ancient Chinese books from the perspective of modern geological science, setting the precedent for the study of the history of geological science in China. Therefore, he is regarded as a great master of China's geological community.

非遗文化
Intangible Cultural Heritage

荻港民间丝竹 Digang Folk Sizhu

荻港丝竹的历史可追溯到100多年前，所谓“采南浔之丝，载浙北秀竹，传湖地佳音，集弦索精粹，水乡荻港有丝竹者”。荻港民间丝竹是和孚镇特有的，用二胡、弦子、月琴、横笛、竹箫、小锣、响铃、木鱼等器乐，以吹、拉、弹、唱等方式，演奏各种民间小调、戏曲及现代流行歌曲。演奏者不需要化装，不需要道具，不需要服装，也不限场地，只要几只条凳坐下来即可演奏。

The history of Digang Sizhu (a popular music in Jiangnan: Si stands for string instruments, while Zhu stands for bamboo instruments) can be traced back to more than 100 years ago. The local Sizhu in Digang is unique to Hefu Town. It uses Erhu, Xianzi, moon guitar, fife, bamboo flute, small gong, diabolo, wooden fish and other music instruments, with various ways of playing, such as blowing, pulling, playing and singing, when it comes to perform folk tunes, Chinese traditional operas and modern pop songs. There are no needs for makeup, props, costumes, or space restrictions, a few stools are the only precondition for a nice Digang Sizhu performance.

农业文化
Agricultural Culture

湖州桑基鱼塘系统 Huzhou Mulberry-Based-Fishpond Ecosystem

紧依在古运河之畔的古村养鱼可追溯至吴越时期，千百年来，这里的人们种桑养蚕、捕鱼养鱼，繁衍生息。他们在劳动中发明、发展了“塘基上种桑、桑叶喂蚕、蚕沙养鱼、鱼粪肥塘、塘泥壅桑”的桑基鱼塘生态模式。湖州桑基鱼塘系统位于浙江省湖州市南浔区西部。现有6万亩桑地和15万亩鱼塘，是中国传统桑基鱼塘系统中最集中、最大、保留最完整的区域。2014年，湖州桑基鱼塘系统被我国农业部(今农业农村部)认定为中国重要农业文化遗产。

The ancient fishing industry near the Beijing-Hangzhou Grand Canal can be traced back to the period of Wu and Yue. For thousands of years, people here lived their lives by developing mulberry planting, sericulture, fish farming, etc. In their work, they invented and developed the mulberry pond ecological model of “planting mulberry on the pond foundation, feeding silkworms with mulberry leaves, raising fish with silkworm excrement”. Huzhou mulberry-based-fishpond ecosystem is located in the west of Nanxun District, Huzhou City, Zhejiang Province. There are

60,000 mu of mulberry land and 150,000 mu of fish ponds, which are the most concentrated, largest, and most intact area in the traditional Chinese mulberry fish pond system. In 2014, it was recognized as China's important agricultural cultural heritage by the Ministry of Agriculture (now the Ministry of Agriculture and Rural Affairs) of the People's Republic of China.

文化寻踪之出行提示 Travel tips

寻踪之旅载体:鱼文化节

寻踪之旅地点:浙江省湖州市南浔区和孚镇荻港村

寻踪之旅时间:通常为1月

寻踪信息查询:(1)http://www.nanxun.gov.cn/;(2)"南浔发布"微信公众平台;(3)搜狐、腾讯等多家网站。

Cultural Activity: Fish Culture Festival

Ancient Village: Digang Village, Hefu Town, Nanxun District, Huzhou City, Zhejiang Province

Travel Time: Usually in January

For More Information: (1) Please visit http://www.nanxun.gov.cn/; (2) Please search on the WeChat public platform "Nanxun Fabu"; (3) Please visit the websites such as Sohu, Tencent, etc.

参考资料

http://www.nanxun.gov.cn/art/2016/2/2/art_1229211167_54850869.html
https://zjnews.zjol.com.cn/zjnews/huzhounews/201705/t20170508_3574035.

shtml

http://nync.huzhou.gov.cn/art/2021/3/22/art_1229209233_58925183.html

http://zj.people.com.cn/GB/187016/389537/

https://hzdaily.hangzhou.com.cn/hzrb/2017/05/08/article_detail_1_20170508A075.html

http://www.tourzj.gov.cn/play/vdestination_zixun.aspx

http://bbs.zol.com.cn/dcbbs/d17_24207.html

https://news.gujianchina.cn/show-891.html

https://www.sohu.com/a/163129077_643840

http://www.tourzj.gov.cn/play/vdestination_zixun.aspx

https://www.sohu.com/a/163129077_643840

http://jingguan.yuanlin.com/scene/building/2017-6-9/28200.html

http://www.zjich.cn/xiangmu/xiangmushow.html?id=2253

http://www.zj.gov.cn/art/2019/9/6/art_1676281_37812046.html

2月 February

文化活动一：正月十四元宵行会
Cultural Activity (1): The Lantern Festival Parade

文化活动二：元宵节
Cultural Activity (2): The Lantern Festival

文化活动三：『台阁』年俗文化节
Cultural Activity (3): Taige New Year Folk Culture Festival

文化活动四：观海卫都神行会
Cultural Activity (4): Dushen Parade in Guanhaiwei Town

文化活动五：武义抬阁
Cultural Activity (5): Wuyi Taige

文化活动一:正月十四元宵行会

Cultural Activity (1): The Lantern Festival Parade

文化寻踪之浙里村落 Ancient Towns

➢ 宁海县前童镇

Qiantong Town, Ninghai County

前童镇,地处浙江省宁波市宁海县西南,面积68平方公里,人口2.6万,是浙东地区保存至今的最具儒家文化古韵的小镇,现存1300多间各式古建民居。这里,“家家有雕梁,户户有活水”。

Qiantong Town is located in the southwest of Ninghai County, Ningbo City, Zhejiang Province. With a population of 26,000, it covers an area of 68 square kilometers, and is the town with the most ancient Confucian culture in eastern Zhejiang. Besides, there are still more than 1,300 well-preserved ancient dwellings. As the saying goes, “every family has carved beams, and every household has running water" in Qiantong.

文化寻踪之浙里印记 Cultural Imprints

➢ 非遗文化 Intangible Cultural Heritage

正月十四元宵行会 The Lantern Festival Parade

前童正月十四元宵行会是一种古老的民俗游艺活动，至今已有500多年的历史。主要以鸣群锣、抬鼓亭、舞狮子、放铳花等方式来表现。一是纪念祖先的功德，祈求丰年；二是通过行会，聚集民心兴修水利，做好春耕准备工作；三是传承水利管理的责任。宁海传统习俗是在正月十四过元宵节，于是行会巡游也成了前童一年中最热闹、最欢乐的时光。

The Lantern Festival Parade in Qiantong is an ancient folk entertainment activity with a history of more than 500 years. It is mainly performed by beating gongs, lifting drum pavilions, lion dance, and setting off firecrackers. The parade is held for several reasons: first, to commemorate the merits of the ancestors and pray for good harvest; second, to entertain the common people and remind them of the coming water conservancy and spring plowing; third, to inherit the responsibility of water management. The Ninghai locals keep the tradition to celebrate the Lantern Festival on the fourteenth of the first lunar month, so the parade has also become the most exciting and happiest time of the whole year.

十里红妆 Ten-*Li* Red Dowry

十里红妆是宁海和浙东地区特有的传统婚妆系列及相关民俗。当地嫁女的嫁妆，大到床铺家具，小到针头线脑，一应俱全。迎嫁妆队伍浩浩荡荡，绵延十里，十分气派。十里红妆规模声势之大，数量之多，门类之齐全，制作工艺之精湛，艺术价值之高，耗费之昂贵，均为全国罕见。十里红妆主要包括婚嫁仪式中的“迎嫁妆”习俗和红妆器物的制作工艺传承两部分。宁海十里红妆婚俗是江南婚姻民俗的重要组成部分，它集中体现了江南手工技艺的特色，表达了喜庆、吉祥的美好祝愿，反映出江南人民积极乐观的生活态度。

Ten-*Li* Red Dowry is the traditional wedding customs unique to Ninghai and eastern Zhejiang. The dowry for the local marrying-girls ranges from beds, furniture to small needles. The welcoming dowry team is so mighty that it may stretch ten *li*. Its scale, number, complete range, exquisite craftsmanship, high artistic value, and high cost are all rare in the country. The dowry mainly includes two parts: the tradition of “welcoming the dowry” in the wedding ceremony and the production process of wedding utensils. The wedding custom of Ninghai is an important part of marriage folklore. It embodies the characteristics of the handicrafts in the south of the Yangtze River, expresses happy and auspicious wishes, and reflects the positive and optimistic life attitude of the local people.

➢ 建筑文化
Architectural Culture

八卦水系 The Bagua Water System

1508年，浙东大旱，庄稼颗粒无收，童濠率村民坚持数年修筑杨柳洪碶，引白溪水入村。当时的人根据整个村子的地理形状，依照“太极生两仪、两仪生四象、四象生八卦”的原理，将水渠一分二、二分四、四分八，依地势顺路沿屋流淌，最终形成了家家户户、门前屋后、小桥流水、清流映带的八卦水系。从村口牌坊进入，顺着水流漫步在鹅卵石小径，一眼望去，可以发现每条街道墙弄的路边都有一条渠道，渠里清水汩汩流着，犹如一条玉带飘荡穿梭在古镇。

In 1508, there was a severe drought in eastern Zhejiang, which resulted in no harvest of crops. Under the leadership of Tong Hao, the villagers worked hard on the Bai Rivulet water diversion project. According to the geographical condition, the people at that time divided the canal into two, two into four, and four into eight using the Taoist cosmology, a religious, philosophical and ritual tradition of Chinese origin. Running along the houses according to the terrain, the Bagua or Eight Diagrams water system benefits every household. Entering from the memorial archway at the entrance of the village, strolling along the cobblestone path, you can see a channel along the roadside of each alley, and the clear water in the channel is gurgling like a jade belt floating through the ancient town.

文化寻踪之出行提示 Travel tips

寻踪之旅载体:正月十四元宵行会

寻踪之旅地点:浙江省宁波市宁海县前童镇

寻踪之旅时间:通常为2月

寻踪信息查询:(1)http://www.ninghai.gov.cn/;(2)"前童发布"微信公众平台;(3)搜狐、腾讯等多家网站。

Cultural Activity: The Lantern Festival Parade

Ancient Town: Qiantong Town, Ninghai County, Ningbo City, Zhejiang Province

Travel Time: Usually in February

For More Information: (1) Please visit http://www.ninghai.gov.cn/; (2) Please search on the WeChat public platform "Qiantong Fabu"; (3) Please visit the websites such as Suhu, Tencent, etc.

参考资料

https://www.sohu.com/a/212601890_349170

https://www.ihningbo.cn/news/show/2085

http://www.zjich.cn/xiangmu/xiangmushow.html?id=1711

http://www.ninghai.gov.cn/art/2021/5/8/art_1229092947_59027623.html

http://www.zjich.cn/news/newsshow.html?id=441830

http://www.zjich.cn/news/newsshow.html?id=440475

http://www.zjich.cn/zaiti/zaitishow.html?id=377

http://usa.chinadaily.com.cn/epaper/2011-04/22/content_12377179.htm

https://www.sohu.com/a/223002649_747909
http://www.zjich.cn/xiangmu/xiangmushow.html?id=284
https://www.ihningbo.cn/directory/show/19
http://www.taihainet.com/lifeid/culture/whdht/202001/2348612.html
http://www.ihchina.cn/Article/Index/detail?id=15237
https://xw.qq.com/cmsid/20200519A0Q6NO00
https://www.sohu.com/a/203810825_747909
http://www.ninghai.gov.cn/art/2020/8/20/art_1229235505_54661906.html
http://nh.cnnb.com.cn/system/2017/11/08/011620281.shtml

文化活动二：元宵节

Cultural Activity (2): The Lantern Festival

文化寻踪之浙里村落 Ancient Towns

嵊州市崇仁镇

Chongren Town, Shengzhou City

浙江省嵊州市崇仁镇，位于嵊州市西北部，离市区11千米，是一个美丽幽静的江南古镇，素有"浙东小上海"之称。崇仁镇，距今已有近千年的历史，原名杏花村。北宋熙宁年间，受皇帝敕封的义门裘氏从婺州分迁此地，裘氏以崇尚仁义为本，故名其地为崇仁。古镇至今仍保留着庞大的古建筑群，具有宋朝遗风、明清特色。

Chongren Town is located in the northwest of Shengzhou City, Zhejiang Province, 11 kilometers away from the urban area. It is a beautiful and quiet ancient town in the south of the Yangtze River, reputed as "Little Shanghai in East Zhejiang". Formerly known as Xinghua Village, the town enjoys a history of nearly a thousand years. During the reign of Emperor Xining in the Northern Song Dynasty, the Qiu family, who was entrusted by the emperor, moved here from Wuzhou (today's Jinhua). Qiu's family advocated benevolence and righteousness as their foundation belief, so they named the town "Chongren" meaning benevolence and righteousness. The ancient town still retains a huge group of ancient buildings, with the relics of the Song Dynasty and the characteristics of the Ming and Qing Dynasties.

文化寻踪之浙里印记 Cultural Imprints

建筑文化 Architectural Culture

崇仁古建筑群 Ancient Construction Complex in Chongren

步入崇仁，从明代至民国的古建筑群序列完整，类型丰富。群内庙宇、祠堂、古戏台、民居、牌坊、药铺、店房、桥梁、池塘、水井一应俱全。以玉山公祠为中心，保存完整的老台门就有100余座，台门之间用跨街小楼勾连，既珠联璧合，又独立成章，体现了“分户合族、聚只一家”的遗风。崇仁镇建造工艺讲究、独特，从选址到建设，从建筑到街道格局，从功能结构到空间结构，从基础设施到防御体系，布局合理，结构完备。

In Chongren, the ancient construction complex from the Ming Dynasty to the Republic of China is complete and rich in types. There are a variety of constructions available including the temples, ancestral halls, ancient stage, folk houses, memorial archways, drug stores, bridges, ponds, and wells, etc. With Yushan Ancestral Hall as the center, there are more than 100 well-preserved ancient Taimens (a typical Shaoxing residential unit), which are connected by cross-street buildings. They are both perfectly united and relatively independent, reflecting the ancestors' living concept that "be an individual household while separated; be a whole big family while united". The construction technique of Chongren Town is exquisite and unique, speaking of the varied weighing dimensions including site selection, construction, architecture quality, street layout, functional structure, spatial structure, infrastructure, defense system, etc.

玉山公祠 Yushan Ancestral Hall

玉山公祠是宗祠建筑的杰出代表，以建筑考究、砖石木雕刻精美著称。它坐北朝南，占地面积1012平方米。公祠分三进，依纵轴线布局，自南向北有照壁、天井、门厅、戏台、正大殿、过道、后大殿，戏台天井两侧有厢房各五间。玉山公祠的木雕、石雕、砖雕工艺精湛，件数之多，数嵊州宗祠之最，堪称一绝。

Yushan Ancestral Hall is an excellent representative of ancestral constructions, famous for its exquisite architecture, stone carvings and wood carvings. Sitting in the north and facing south, the hall covers an area of 1,012 square meters, with three rows of constructions. Along the vertical axis from south to north, there are Zhaobi (a screen wall facing the gate of a house), patio, entrance hall, stage, main hall, corridors, and back hall. On both sides of the stage and patio there are five wing rooms respectively. The woodcarving, stone carving, and brick carvings in Yushan Ancestral Hall are delicate in technique, and large in scale, which make it the most outstanding representative among Shengzhou ancestral halls.

➢ 非遗文化
Intangible Cultural Heritage

大头荷 Datouhe

大头荷，又名大头和，清咸丰、同治年间，人们为了活跃文化生活，在彩头戏“掘藏”的基础上，把面具（俗称“木脸”）改作“头套”，因为头套特大，没有头发，像和尚的头，故称大头和。其创始人费德风为浙江嵊州市崇仁镇赵马村人。大头荷初创时期有36个包括生旦净末不同行当不同脸谱的大头荷。至民国初，演变成9个头套的“八仙庆寿”，作为喜庆节庆时的开场戏，祈求风调雨顺，延年益寿。

In the reign of Emperor Xianfeng and Emperor Tongzhi of the Qing Dynasty, people changed their masks (commonly known as wooden faces) into “headgears” adapted from traditional operas in order to activate cultural life. Without hair, the headgear is like extra-large monk’s head, so it is called Datouhe (similar with “a big head” in sound). Its founder Fei Defeng was from Chongren Town. During the initial period, there were 36 different Datouhes representing various types of roles in traditional Chinese operas. At the beginning of the Republic of China, the number of Datouhe changed into 9, mainly used to perform “Eight Immortals (in the legend) Offering Birthday Celebration”, which served as the opening activity of the festive season, praying for good weather and longevity.

越剧 Yue Opera

越剧，中国第二大剧种，有第二国剧之称，又被称为“流传最广的地方剧种”，亦为中国五大戏曲剧种之一。越剧发源于浙江嵊州，发祥于上海，繁荣于全国，在发展中汲取了昆曲、话剧、绍剧等特色剧种之大成，经历了由男子越剧到女子越剧为主的历史性演变。越剧长于抒情，以唱为主，声音优美动听，表演真切动人，唯美典雅，极具江南灵秀之气。2006年5月20日，越剧经国务院批准列入第一批国家级非物质文化遗产名录。

Yue Opera, the second largest opera genre in China, is also known as the second national opera, and the “most widely spread local opera genre”, included in the five major opera genres in China. It originated in Shengzhou, Zhejiang, flourished in Shanghai, and spread throughout the country. Yue Opera has absorbed the great achievements of Kunqu Opera, modern drama, Shao Opera and other characteristic operas, and has experienced a historical evolution from male performance to female performance. With beautiful singing and elegant performance, Yue Opera is good at expressing emotion, presenting the charm of life in the south of the Yantze River. On May 20, 2006, Yue Opera was approved by the State Council to be included in the first batch of national intangible cultural heritage lists.

文化寻踪之出行贴士 Travel Tips

寻踪之旅载体：元宵节

寻踪之旅地点：浙江省嵊州市崇仁镇

寻踪之旅时间：通常为2月

寻踪信息查询：(1)http://sznews.zjol.com.cn/；(2)“嵊州发布”微信公众平台；(3)搜狐、腾讯等多家网站。

Cultural Activity: The Lantern Festival

Ancient Town: Chongren Town, Shengzhou City, Zhejiang Province

Travel Time: Usually in February

For More Information: (1) Please visit http://sznews.zjol.com.cn/; (2) Please search on the WeChat public platform “Shengzhou Fabu”; (3) Please visit the websites such as Sohu, Tencent, etc.

参考资料

https://www.douban.com/note/725492904/

http://www.zjich.cn/news/newsshow.html?id=433629

http://sznews.zjol.com.cn/sznews/system/2019/12/18/032074619.shtml

http://www.zjich.cn/xiangmu/xiangmushow.html?id=1055

http://travel.sina.com.cn/china/2014-05-05/1832261000_2.shtml

http://sznews.zjol.com.cn/sznews/system/2019/02/27/031484202.shtml

http://www.sx.gov.cn/art/2018/9/25/art_1462938_21536703.html

http://www.zjich.cn/xiangmu/xiangmushow.html?id=1526

http://www.zjich.cn/xiangmu/xiangmulist.html?keyword=%u8D8A%u5267

http://www.szxq.com/zixun/yju/yuejuzixun/201601/15-18310.html

文化活动三:"台阁"年俗文化节

Cultural Activity (3): Taige New Year Folk Culture Festival

文化寻踪之浙里村落 Ancient Towns

➢ 诸暨市枫桥镇

Fengqiao Town, Zhuji City

枫桥镇位于诸暨市东部,是诸暨市的第一人口、地域大镇。枫桥镇以枫溪得名,作为地名始于隋朝的枫桥驿,自后,一直为诸暨东北部政治经济文化中心。枫桥历来为浙江省历史文化名镇,"枫桥经验""枫桥衬衫""枫桥香榧"闻名全国。

Located in the east of Zhuji City, Fengqiao Town is the the city's most populous and geographically large town. It is named after the Feng Brook, and was officially in use due to the Fengqiao courier station in the Sui Dynasty. Since then, the town has been the political, economic and cultural center of the northeast of Zhuji. Fengqiao has always been a famous historical and cultural town in Zhejiang Province, and its "Fengqiao Experience", "Fengqiao Shirt" and "Fengqiao Torreya" are well-known throughout the country.

文化寻踪之浙里印记 Cultural Imprints

➤ 名人文化 Celebrity Culture

王冕故地 Hometown of Wang Mian

王冕(1310—1359年),浙江省绍兴市诸暨枫桥人,元朝著名画家、诗人、篆刻家。他出身贫寒,幼年替人放牛,靠自学成才。王冕性格孤傲,鄙视权贵,诗作多为同情人民苦难、谴责豪门权贵、轻视功名利禄、描写田园隐逸生活之作。他一生爱好梅花,种梅、咏梅,又攻画梅。王冕一生的大部分时间隐居在山明水秀的诸暨枫桥镇北九里山的水南村。朴实的生活与清幽的山水孕育了他热爱生活、热爱劳动人民的性格,赋予他的诗画创作以浓厚的生活气息。

Wang Mian (1310-1359), a native of Fengqiao, Zhuji, Shaoxing City, Zhejiang Province, was a famous painter, poet, and expert in seal cutting of the Yuan Dynasty. He was born in a poor family, grazing cattle for others at a young age, and grew up by self-taught. Wang Mian was aloof and arrogant and despises the powerful. His poems sympathized with the suffering of the people, condemned the rich and powerful, despised fame and wealth, and described the pastoral life in seclusion. He loved plum blossoms, planting plums, chanting plums, and painting plums all his life.

For most of his life, Wang Mian lived in seclusion in Shuinan Village, Fengqiao Town. The simple life and quiet landscape gave birth to his love of life and appreciation for working people, and gave his poetry and paintings a strong vitality from life.

枫桥三贤 The Three Sages of Fengqiao

元末至清初三百年间，诸暨这块古越大地，孕育了王冕、杨维桢、陈洪绶三位名士，诸暨人尊称他们为“三贤”。枫桥三贤以其精湛的艺术造诣而在中国书法史、绘画史乃至整个中国文化史中留下了浓墨重彩的一笔。王冕首创花乳石刻印与“胭脂没骨梅”的画法；杨维桢首创“铁崖体”诗风与“西湖竹枝词”的民歌体；陈洪绶自创对比夸张的人物画风格，成了海派人物画的开山大师。

During the three hundred years from the end of the Yuan Dynasty to the beginning of the Qing Dynasty, the ancient land of Zhuji gave birth to three celebrities, Wang Mian, Yang Weizhen, and Chen Hongshou, who were later called “Three Sages” by the Zhuji people. With their superb artistic attainments, the three celebrities left a strong mark in the history of Chinese calligraphy, painting and even the history of Chinese culture. Wang Mian pioneered a new seal cutting technique and the painting method of “Drawing Boneless Plum with Rouge”; Yang Weizhen pioneered the “Tieya” poetic style and the “West Lake Bamboo Branch Poetry” folk song style; Chen Hongshou created the contrasting and exaggerated figure painting style, who was regarded as the “Originator of Shanghai Style Figure Painting”.

➢ 非遗文化
Intangible Cultural Heritage

台阁 Taige

台阁是一种历史悠久、分布广泛的民俗表演，它起于南宋，明清发展繁盛，明代绍兴文人张岱就在《陶庵梦忆》中记载了枫桥杨神庙迎台阁的盛况。为缅怀过去，留住乡愁，诸暨市枫桥镇在1月底或2月初举办“台阁市”年俗文化节，重现南宋时期的繁华景象。喝黄酒、看舞狮、买年货、新年祈福，一场独具地方特色的文化盛宴让古镇弥漫着浓浓的年味。

Taige, the pavilion carrying ritual, is a kind of folk performance with a long history and wide distribution. It began in the Southern Song Dynasty and developed prosperously during the Ming and Qing Dynasties. Shaoxing literati Zhang Dai in the Ming Dynasty recorded the grand occasion of pavilion welcoming in Fengqiao God Yang's Temple in *Tao'an Dream Memory*. In order to remember the past and retain the nostalgia, Fengqiao Town of Zhuji City held the Taige New Year Culture Festival at the end of January or early February of the lunar calendar to reproduce the prosperous scene of the Southern Song Dynasty. Drinking rice wine, watching lion dances, purchasing new year goods, and praying for the lunar new year, a cultural feast with unique local characteristics fills the ancient town with a strong flavor of the year.

文化寻踪之出行贴士 Travel Tips

寻踪之旅载体:"台阁"年俗文化节

寻踪之旅地点:浙江省诸暨市枫桥镇

寻踪之旅时间:通常为2月

寻踪信息查询:(1)http://www.zhuji.gov.cn/;(2)"诸暨发布"微信公众平台;(3)搜狐、腾讯等多家网站。

Cultural Activity: Taige New Year Folk Culture Festival

Ancient Town: Fengqiao Town, Zhuji City, Zhejiang Province

Travel Time: Usually in February

For More Information: (1) Please visit http://www. zhuji. gov. cn/; (2) Please search on the WeChat public platform "Zhuji Fabu"; (3) Please visit the websites such as Sohu, Tencent, etc.

参考资料

http://kuaibao.qq.com/s/20191208A0L7SX00
http://www.zsbeike.com/tp/7415890.html
https://www.douban.com/note/616964443/?type=collect
http://www.zjich.cn/news/newsshow.html?id=441769
https://baijiahao.baidu.com/s?id=1623712194297410008&wfr=spider&for=pc
https://www.sxqunwen.com/areanews/4029.html
http://www.zhuji.gov.cn/art/2020/10/10/art_1229074735_59016469.html
https://www.thepaper.cn/newsDetail_forward_5530558
http://www.jrzj.cn/art/2019/3/18/art_18_2100.html

https://m.sohu.com/a/271032924_100166591

http://travel.sina.com.cn/china/2014-02-26/1419250223.shtml

文化活动四:观海卫都神行会

Cultural Activity (4): Dushen Parade in Guanhaiwei Town

文化寻踪之浙里村落 Ancient Towns

➢ 慈溪市观海卫镇鸣鹤古镇

Minghe, Guanhaiwei Town, Cixi City

鸣鹤古镇位于慈溪市观海卫镇南部,是一个千年古镇,物华天宝、人杰地灵,是慈溪市唯一的省级历史文化名镇。古镇依山成街、因河成镇、镇边有寺,渔耕人家枕河而居。鸣鹤其名字的由来与唐初时当地虞氏望族有关。唐代大书法家虞世南的孙子虞九皋,字鸣鹤,青少年时文才便为人们所推重。在唐元和年间(806—820),虞九皋中进士,可惜及第不久后,在长安英年早逝,家乡人为纪念他,就用他的字“鸣鹤”来命名这里。

Minghe Ancient Town is located in the south of Guanhaiwei Town, Cixi City. It is a thousand-year-old town with rich resources and outstanding people, and also the only provincial-level historical and cultural town in Cixi City. The ancient street were built backing the mountains, and the ancient town came into being became of the river. Near the town is an ancient temple, and the local fishermen and farmers dwell alongside the riverbank. The origin of the town name Minghe was related to the local distinguished Yu family in the early Tang Dynasty. The grandson of the great calligrapher Yu Shinan, named Yu Jiugao, also known as Minghe, was highly admired as a teenager because of his talents. In the reign of Emperor Yuanhe of the Tang Dynasty, he was awarded as the presented scholar. Unfortunately, he died young in the capital city, Chang'an, not long after. In memory of him, people named his hometown after his name "Minghe".

文化寻踪之浙里印记 Cultural Imprints

建筑文化
Architectural Culture

金仙寺 Jinxian Temple

金仙寺初建于佛教鼎盛时期——南朝梁大同年间，至今已有1400余年的历史。其背靠隐山，面临白洋湖，素有“以山而兼湖之胜”的美誉。1942年，浙东抗日武装在金仙寺成立了第三战区三北游击司令部，寺院成为抗日活动的重要场所。绕山环湖的名胜古迹，造就了鸣鹤当时的辉煌。

Jinxian Temple was first built during the heyday of Buddhism, that is, the reign of Emperor Datong of the Liang Dynasty in the Southern Dynasties, and has a history of more than 1,400 years. Backed by hidden mountains and facing the Baiyang Lake, Jinxian Temple is known as "a combining beauties of both mountains and lakes". In 1942, the East Zhejiang Anti-Japanese Armed Forces established the Third North Guerrilla No. 3 North Headquarters at Jinxian Temple, which became an important place for anti-Japanese activities during the special period. The historical sites surrounding the mountains and lakes created the glory of Minghe at that time.

24间走马楼 Zoumalou with Twenty-Four Rooms

24间走马楼是嘉庆十四年间国药巨商叶心培之子叶赐凤所建，距今已有200多年的历史，该宅共7间2弄2层，有24间之多，并且楼屋四周都有走廊可通行，甚至可以在里面畅通无阻地骑马。楼内部做工细致，枋柱上刻有花卉、鸳鸯、花篮等表示吉祥如意的装饰，门窗、扶梯都用花格，墙上有砖制花窗、龙凤、蝙蝠图案，所以有"回廊挂落花格窗"之说。

Zoumalou with twenty-four rooms was built by Ye Cifeng, the son of Ye Xinpei, a giant Chinese medicine merchant in the 14th year of Emperor Jiaqing, boasting a history of more than 200 years. The mansion has 7 rooms, 2 lanes and 2 floors, totaling 24 rooms all around, all connected by the corridors which are so spacious that even horseback riding inside can be realized. The interior of the mansion was meticulous in workmanship, and the pillars were engraved with flowers, mandarin ducks, flower baskets and other auspicious decorations. Doors, windows, and staircases were all decorated with lattices, while the walls were decorated with brick windows and patterns of dragons and phoenixes.

银号 Shen's Mansion

银号，又称沈氏大屋，是两层多进院落式走马楼。整个建筑面积约1855平方米，屋共三进，每进五间，呈狭长形。此屋主人姓沈，沈氏先人曾在北京开银楼，积财后捐官，故可在此建五马山墙大屋。银号门头隽朗优雅，砖雕门楼上书有"云渚分华"四字，内中正厅张贴着清光绪辰年(1892年)沈祖梁高中秀才的捷报，向我们传递着当时主人的气魄和辉煌。

Shen's Mansion is a two-floor court-yard type buildings with a wingding corridor. The entire construction area is about 1,855 square meters, and has three rows of constructions, five rooms each, which are narrow and long. The owner of this mansion was surnamed Shen, whose ancestor earned a large sum of money in Beijing, and became an official afterwards, so he was allowed to build five-horse-head shaped gabble walls. The mansion gate is delicate and elegant, with the four Chinese characters "Yun Zhu Fen Hua" carved on the arch. The main hall is posted with a piece of good news report when their ancestor Shen Zuliang was awarded Xiucai, a title awarded to graduates of a type of state examination in 1892, which still depicts the owner's glory at the time.

非遗文化 Intangible Cultural Heritage

观海卫都神行会 Dushen Parade in Guanhaiwei Town

都神殿始建于明末清初，位于慈溪市观海卫镇锦堂村蛤蜊山，是当地最有影响力的民间信仰活动场所之一。都神行会是浙东观海卫都神殿的传统庙会，迎请五都大帝出殿行会的民间祈福文艺巡游活动。都神行会

的历史，可追溯到乾隆四十四年。当时“五姓一柱”（林家、吴家、韩家、徐家、蒋家称为“五姓”，方家称为“一柱”）20余个自然村的老百姓自发组织“都神会”，祈求国泰民安、风调雨顺。如今，都神行会成了慈溪民俗文化的缩影。

First built in the late Ming and early Qing Dynasties, and located in Mountain Geli, Guanhaiwei Town, Cixi City, Dushen Temple is one of the most influential places for folk belief activities among the locals. Dushen parade, the five gods' parade, is a traditional temple fair in East Zhejiang, held mainly for the blessings and entertainment. The history of the parade can be traced back to the forty-fourth year of the reign of Emperor Qianlong in the Qing Dynasty. At that time, more than 20 villages spontaneously organized the "Dushen Parade", praying for the prosperity of the country and the people. Now, the parade has become the epitome of Cixi' folk culture.

宁波走书 Ningbo Zoushu

宁波走书又名莲花文书、犁铧文书，流行于浙江省宁波市及周边地区。它起源于清代同治、光绪年间，经历代艺人的加工而逐步发展成形。宁波走书的表演先后经历了三个发展阶段，最初是一人演出的“坐唱”，由一名演员边唱边操乐器自行伴奏；其后演变为“里走书”，即一人坐于桌后演唱，一人坐在桌子横旁伴奏；再后演唱者与伴奏者分坐桌子两旁，演唱者可在台上走动表演，称为“外走书”。

Ningbo Zoushu, is popular in Ningbo City and its surrounding areas.

It originated in the reign of Emperor Tongzhi and Emperor Guangxu of the Qing Dynasty, and gradually developed and formed through the processing of contemporary artists. The performance of Ningbo Zoushu has gone through three stages of development. At first, it was a one-person "sitting and singing", performed by one single actor while singing and playing a musical instrument; then it evolved into "Lizoushu", with one person sitting behind the table singing, and another person sitting beside the table to accompany; then the singer and accompanist sit on both sides of the table separately, and the singer can walk around the stage to perform, which is called "Waizoushu".

越窑青瓷烧制技艺 Yue Kiln Celadon Firing Technique

越窑青瓷始烧于东汉，原始瓷到成熟青瓷的演变就在越窑的龙窑里完成，因此，上林湖越窑青瓷也被称为"母亲瓷"。越窑延续烧制千年，于北宋末南宋初衰落，是我国延续时间最长、影响范围广泛、内涵相当丰富的窑系。越窑的制瓷技艺水平、装饰工艺和造型水极其成熟，成为其他瓷窑模仿借鉴和引进之对象，是中国古代青瓷瓷窑的代表之一。

Yue kiln celadon was first fired in the Eastern Han Dynasty. The evolution from primitive porcelain to mature celadon was successfully completed in the dragon kiln of Yue kiln. Therefore, Shanglin Lake Yue kiln celadon is also called "the mother porcelain". Yue kilns lasted for thousands of years and declined at the end of the Northern Song Dynasty and the beginning of the Southern Song Dynasty. They are the longest-lasting kilns in China, with a wide range of influence and quite rich connotations. Yue kiln is mature in porcelain-making skills, decoration craftsmanship and modeling level, thus it has become the object of imitation and introduction of other kilns, and one of the representatives of ancient Chinese celadon kilns.

➢ 红色文化
Red Culture

宓大昌大屋 Mi Dachang House

宓大昌大屋,位于慈溪市观海卫镇昌明村宓家埭街18号,是全国重点文物保护单位。宓大昌大屋原是清代中叶在杭州经营烟叶的宓彰孝旧宅,是一座具有江南独特风韵的口字型四合院。

Mi Dachang House, located at No. 18 Mijiadai Street, Changming Village, Guanhaiwei Town, Cixi City, is a national key cultural relics protection unit. Mi Dachang House was originally the old house of Mi Zhangxiao who managed tobacco business in Hangzhou in the middle of the Qing Dynasty. It is a mouth-shaped courtyard with a unique charm of southern China.

文化寻踪之出行贴士 Travel Tips

寻踪之旅载体:观海卫都神行会

寻踪之旅地点:浙江省慈溪市观海卫镇鸣鹤古镇

寻踪之旅时间:通常为2月

寻踪信息查询:(1)http://www.cnnb.com.cn/;(2)“观海卫发布”微信公众平台;(3)搜狐、腾讯等多家网站。

Cultural Activity: Dushen Parade in Guanhaiwei Town

Ancient Town: Minghe, Guanhaiwei Town, Cixi City, Zhejiang Province

Travel Time: Usually in February

For More Information: (1) Please visit http://www. cnnb. com. cn/; (2) Please search on the WeChat public platform "Guanhaiwei Fabu"; (3) Please visit the websites soch as Sohu, Tencent, etc.

参考资料

http://www.nbwb.net/pd_mcbh/info.aspx?Id=47897

https://www.meipian.cn/2hpaivz0

http://nbcxghw.zjzwfw.gov.cn/col/col997478/index.html

https://www.sohu.com/a/331058868_119016

http://travel.sina.com.cn/china/2014-11-04/0927283409_3.shtml

https://www.sohu.com/a/353253310_119016

https://www.meipian.cn/36rgeivd

https://www.sohu.com/a/125626086_395075

http://news.cnnb.com.cn/system/2019/02/17/030028083.shtml

https://www.sohu.com/a/443162165_100034535

http://www.ihchina.cn/project_details/13698/

http://www.zgdazxw.com.cn/culture/2015-09/02/content_87120.htm

http://dzb.cnxsg.cn/html/2020-09/08/content_74025_12349936.htm

http://daily.cnnb.com.cn/nbwb/html/2010-08/08/content_221399.htm

https://www.nbdaj.gov.cn/zy/nbjy/lswh/202008/t20200828_30904.shtml

https://xw.qq.com/cmsid/20210427A09UGP00

http://daily.cnnb.com.cn/nbwb/html/2012-08/21/content_513403.htm

https://www.sohu.com/a/239334864_726586

http://www.cnnb.com.cn/xinwen/system/2020/08/31/030184225.shtml

文化活动五：武义抬阁

Cultural Activity (5): Wuyi Taige

文化寻踪之浙里村落 Ancient Villages

➢ 武义县俞源乡俞源村

Yuyuan Village, Yuyuan Town, Wuyi County

俞源村，属浙江省金华市武义县，坐落在武义县西南部，距县城20公里。新近发现明、清古建筑竟有395幢之多，超过有"中国第一古村"之称的江西乐安流坑村。该村以其深厚的文化底蕴，奇异的布局，罕见的古建筑群和精致的木雕、砖雕，以及一个个不解之谜而吸引着国内外众多游客。已有英国、美国、法国、德国、日本、奥地利等13个国家的专家、学者慕名而来。据《俞氏宗谱》，俞源村系明开国皇帝朱元璋的国师刘伯温按天体现象设计的村庄布局建造的。2019年12月25日，国家林业和草原局评价认定俞源乡俞源村为国家森林乡村。

Yuyuan Village belongs to Wuyi County, Jinhua City, Zhejiang Province.

It is located in the southwest of Wuyi County, 20 kilometers away from the county. Recently discovered that there are as many as 395 ancient constructions built in the Ming and Qing Dynasties, surpassing Liukeng Village in Le'an, Jiangxi, which is known as "China's No. 1 ancient village". The village has attracted many tourists from home and abroad with its profound cultural heritage, unique layout, rare ancient buildings, exquisite wood carvings, brick carvings, and unsolved mysteries. Experts and scholars from 13 countries, including Britain, the United States, France, Germany, Japan, and Austria, have come here for research. According to *Genealogy of the Yu Family*, the village of Yu Yuan was built by Liu Bowen, the purohita of the founding emperor Zhu Yuanzhang of the Ming Dynasty, based on the village layout designed by celestial phenomena. On December 25, 2019, the State Forestry and Grassland Administration assessed and recognized Yuyuan Village as a national forest village.

文化寻踪之浙里印记 Cultural Imprints

➢ 建筑文化
Architectural Culture

俞氏宗祠 Yu's Ancestral Hall

明朝嘉靖年间，俞源出了5位名人：俞大有、俞昭、俞款、俞彬、俞世美。当时俞氏家族名声大振，于隆庆元年大兴土木重建俞氏宗祠。宰相严讷赠送"壬林堂"大匾一块。祠堂前后左右六大厅、二小厅，

共51间，占地3176平方米，被誉为“处州第一祠”，祠内雕花戏台，有“金华八县第一台”之美称。

During the reign of Emperor Jiajing of the Ming Dynasty, Yuyuan Village had five celebrities: Yu Dayou, Yu Zhao, Yu Kuan, Yu Bin, and Yu Shimei. At that time, the Yu family's reputation was greatly improved, and their ancestral hall was rebuilt in the first year of the reign of Emperor Longqing. The councellor-in-chief Yan Ne presented a large plaque “Ren Lin Tang”. There are six big halls and two small halls around the ancestral hall, totaling 51 rooms, covering an area of 3,176 square meters. It is known as “the top one ancestral hall in Chuzhou”, and the carved stage in the hall has the reputation of “the top one stage in the eight counties of Jinhua”.

声远堂 Shengyuan Hall

声远堂也称大花厅和六峰堂，由俞继昌建于清康熙二年，共92间，1466平方米。厅堂正对六峰山，地伏全用砖雕，厅内桁条根根浮雕。沿口三根桁条雕三类动物，中间是山上跑的，右边是水中游的。其中九条鲤鱼，活灵活现，会随季节气候的变化而发生黑、黄、红变换，可谓一大奇观。中间的桁条雕有四只麒麟，还有鹿、牛、羊等，称“百兽大梁”。后堂由俞继昌的父亲俞天惠建于明万历四十年，有较高的文物价值。

Shengyuan Hall, also called Dahua Hall or Liufeng Hall, was built by Yu Jichang in the second year of Emperor Kangxi's reign of the Qing Dynasty. It has 92 rooms and 1, 466 square meters in total. Facing Mountain Liufeng, the ground of the hall was carved with bricks, and all the beams were relief carved. Three types of animals were carved along the three beams: the middle one was carved with animals running on the mountain and the right one was carved with those swimming in the water. Among which, nine carps were vividly carved and can change colors among black, yellow and red with the change of seasonal climate, which can be seen as a great spectacle. The beams in the middle were carved with four unicorns, as well as deer, cows, sheep, etc., which are called "beams of all beasts". The back hall was built by Yu Jichang's father Yu Tianhui in the forty years of Emperor Wanli's reign in the Ming Dynasty, which also enjoys a high cultural value.

裕后堂 Yuhou Hall

裕后堂建于清乾隆五十年，原158间，现有120间，占地2560平方米，是全村最大的古屋，故有"大大厅"之称谓。裕后堂的"五无"就是指梁上无灰尘，无蜘蛛结网，无苍蝇、蚊子，无鸟雀过夜栖息过，屋内阴凉好像无夏天。

Yuhou Hall was built in the 50th year of the reign of Emperor Qianlong in the Qing Dynasty, with the covering area of 2,560 square meters. Originally there were 158 rooms and currently there are 120 rooms. It is the largest ancient house in the village, hence it is called "large hall". There is no dust on the beams, no spiders, flies, mosquitoes, and birds have stopped by overnight in Yuhou Hall, and the room is always as cool as if there were no summer.

非遗文化
Intangible Cultural Heritage

武义抬阁 Wuyi Taige

抬阁，俗称"擎台阁"，是武义的一项传统民俗活动，始于清朝康熙末年。抬阁，取当地优质木料制作成台桌，像个小舞台。选村中活泼清秀的童男童女装扮，或用铁棒把小孩顶向高空，摆出腾空动作，经过服装遮隐，似乎小孩是站在枪口刀尖上的古代小英雄，威武勇猛；或把小孩打扮成古代戏曲人物，站在舞台上表演戏曲故事，每桌一个故事场景。每台抬阁由四人抬着游行。俞源抬阁规模庞大，参与者多时达数千人，队伍浩荡，热闹非凡。

"Taige", commonly known as "Lifting Taige", is a traditional folklore activity in Wuyi, which began in the end of Emperor Kangxi's reign of the Qing Dynasty. The locals use local high-quality wood to make a stage-like table, and pick the lively and beautiful children to dress up in costumes, or use an iron rod to push the child up into the sky and make a flying motion. With the covering of the costumes, the mighty and brave children seem ancient heroes standing on the tip of a spear. The children may also be dressed up as the traditional Chinese opera characters, standing on the stage and performing the opera stories, with a story scene at each table. Each "Taige" was carried by four people during the parade. The "Taige" activity in Yuyuan is large in scale and participants, reaching thousands of people at the most.

武义泥水画 Wuyi Plaster Painting

在武义现存的大量明、清及民国建筑中，保留着许许多多的建筑壁

画，因这些壁画大多为泥水匠所画，故当地将之称为“泥水画”。武义泥水画多应用在房屋建筑外墙檐口下、排头尖、马头墙、门楣、窗框、照壁及天井院墙檐口下等部位。武义泥水画的表现形式以水墨为主，有的也施以天然彩色，其艺术效果淡雅朴素，勾勒分明。尤其是画作外框，采用二维和三维几何纹样，装饰效果佳，韵味十足。

In Wuyi's existing constructions of the Ming and Qing Dynasties and the Republic of China, there are many architectural murals. This is because most of these murals were painted by plasterers, they are commonly called "plaster paintings" locally. They are mostly used under the cornices of the exterior walls of houses, the horse-head-shaped walls, the lintels, the window frames, Zhaobi (a screen wall facing the gate of a house), etc. The form of expression of Wuyi plaster paintings is mainly ink and wash painting, and some are also painted in natural colors. The artistic effect is light and simple, and the outline is clear. In particular, the frame of the painting adopts two-dimensional and three-dimensional geometric patterns, which has a good decorative effect and full charm.

文化寻踪之出行贴士 Travel Tips

寻踪之旅载体：武义抬阁

寻踪之旅地点：浙江省金华市武义县俞源乡俞源村

寻踪之旅时间：通常为2月

寻踪信息查询：（1）http://wynews.zjol.com.cn；（2）“武义旅游”微信公

众平台;(3)搜狐、腾讯等多家网站。

Cultural Activity: Wuyi Taige

Ancient Village: Yuyuan Village, Yuyuan Town, Wuyi County, Jinhua City, Zhejiang Province

Travel Time: Usually in February

For More Information: (1) Please visit http://wynews.zjol.com.cn; (2) Please search on the WeChat public platform "Wuyi Lvyou"; (3) Please visit the websites such as Sohu, Tencent, etc.

参考资料

http://wynews.zjol.com.cn/wynews/system/2006/06/15/000357315.shtml
http://blog.sina.com.cn/s/blog_49aa2c640102whut.html
https://www.sohu.com/a/408976345_120799006
https://new.qq.com/rain/a/20210129A06R1U00
http://news.folkw.com/www/qqfs/100914734_4.html
http://wynews.zjol.com.cn/wynews/system/2011/06/17/013881832.shtml
http://www.zjich.cn/xiangmu/xiangmushow.html?id=1167
http://www.zjich.cn/xiangmu/xiangmushow.html?id=1037

3月 March

文化活动一：浙江油菜花节（一）

Cultural Activity (1): Zhejiang Rape Seed Flower Festival I

文化寻踪之浙里村落 Ancient Towns

➢ 仙居县皤滩镇

Potan Town, Xianju County

皤滩镇位于仙居县城西约25千米处，乃永安溪独一无二的五溪汇合点，故皤滩有夜观五月（指五个月亮倒影）之景。皤滩又是水陆交汇之地，沿灵江、永安溪的水路在皤滩拢岸，通往浙西的苍岭古道也在皤滩起步，这种连接东南沿海与浙西内陆的优越地理位置，使它成为古代浙东南山乡的著名商埠和古代食盐之路的重要中转码头。优越的地理位置和极其繁荣的经贸往来，使皤滩成为食盐、布匹、山货等货物的集散地，并逐渐形成别具特色的民间文化。

Potan Town is situated about 25 kilometers away from the west of

Xianju County. It is the unique confluence of the five streams in the Yong'an River, so a unique night view of five moons (referring to the reflection of the five moons) can be seen in the town. Potan is also a place where water and land meet. The waterways along the Lingjiang River and the Yong'an River are merged in Potan, and the ancient Cangling road leading to western Zhejiang also starts in Potan. The superior geographical location connecting the southeast coast and the inland of western Zhejiang facilitated the town to become a famous commercial port in the mountain township of southeastern Zhejiang and an important transit terminal on the ancient salt road. The advantageous geographical location and the prosperous economic and trade exchanges have made Potan a distribution center for salt, cloth, mountain products and other goods, and gradually formed its unique folk culture.

文化寻踪之浙里印记 Cultural Imprints

建筑文化
Architectural Culture

皤滩古建筑群落 Potan Ancient Building Complex

历史上皤滩古镇盐埠民居建筑风格独特，它沿永安溪搭建，蜿蜒曲折，整条古街酷似一条欲腾飞的巨龙。古街上的建筑为典型的江南四合院，连着水埠，方便货物上下。主街道每过几十米就有南北或东西走向的小巷，用于疏通水流或疏散人群，它的科学性在今日看来仍显而易见。徽派建筑中的马头墙则是一道最耀眼的风景线。其建筑种类之多、布局之奇、结构之巧、装饰之美、营造之精，被专家、学者誉为"中国古街文化的博物馆"。

Historically, the salt port dwellings in the ancient town of Potan have a unique architectural style. They were built along the Yong'an River and meandered to create a "long-shaped ancient street", resembling a giant dragon about to take off. The ancient buildings on the street are typical courtyard houses in the south of the Yangtze River. There are alleys running north-south or east-west every tens of meters in the main street, which are used to dredge the water flow or evacuate the crowd. The horse-head-shaped walls in Huizhou-style architecture is the most dazzling landscape. The variety of buildings, the strange layout, the ingenious structure, the beauty of decoration, and the essence of construction have been highly valued by experts, and therefore have been reputed as the "Museum of Chinese Ancient Street Culture".

非遗文化
Intangible Cultural Heritage

仙居花灯 Xianju Lanterns

仙居针刺无骨花灯系因灯面图案由刀凿针刺成孔、灯身无骨而得名，其发源地在浙江省仙居县皤滩。仙居无骨花灯相传始于唐代，俗称"唐灯"，明清时技艺趋于成熟。仙居针刺无骨花灯融绘画、刺绣、建筑艺术于一体，造型别致，空间感强，立面变化丰富，结构细腻生动，具有很高的观赏价值。

Xianju embroidered boneless lanterns got the name because the lamp body is boneless. Its birthplace is in Potan, Xianju County, Zhejiang Province. Legend has it that Xianju boneless lanterns began in the Tang

Dynasty, commonly known as "Tang lanterns", and the making skills became mature in the Ming and Qing Dynasties. Integrating painting, embroidery, and architectural arts, Xianju lanterns are unique in shape, strong in space sense, rich in facade changes, delicate and vivid in structure, with a high aesthetic value.

石窗艺术 Stone Window Art

仙居石窗又称石花窗、石镂窗，是仙居传统民居建筑中普遍使用的石雕构件，是流传于仙居县皤滩与高迁一带的一种传统技艺。明清时，仙居石窗达到鼎盛，技艺日趋成熟、精致。仙居石窗窗花题材丰富，儒、释、道三教文化题材兼容，同时体现仙居民间宗教信仰、生活理想、文化观念和审美趣味，是极其宝贵的非物质文化遗产。

Xianju stone windows, also known as stone flower windows and stone carved windows, are stone carving components commonly used in the traditional residential buildings. It is a traditional technique that has been passed down in Potan and Gaoqian areas. In the Ming and Qing Dynasties, Xianju stone windows developed to a period of great prosperity, and their skills became more mature and refined. The rich themes of Xianju stone windows combine the topics of Confucianism, Buddhism and Taoism, reflecting the religious beliefs, life ideals, cultural perceptions and aesthetic tastes of the locals. It is an extremely valuable intangible cultural heritage for studying the folk culture of Xianju.

文化寻踪之出行贴士 Travel Tips

寻踪之旅载体：浙江油菜花节(一)

寻踪之旅地点：浙江省台州市仙居县皤滩镇

寻踪之旅时间：通常为3月

寻踪信息查询：(1)http://www.taizhou.com.cn；(2)“皤滩古镇”微信公众平台；(3)搜狐、腾讯等多家网站。

Cultural Activity: Zhejiang Rape Seed Flower Festival I

Ancient Town: Potan Town, Xianju County, Taizhou City, Zhejiang Province

Travel Time: Usually in March

For More Information: (1) Please visit http://www.taizhou.com.cn; (2) Please search on the WeChat public platform “Potan Guzhen”; (3) Please visit the websites such as Sohu, Tencent, etc.

参考资料

http://www.zjtz.gov.cn/art/2010/9/10/art_1229049728_52491673.html
https://www.gujianchina.cn/quote/show-137.html
http://nh.cnnb.com.cn/system/2014/03/07/010909159.shtml
http://www.taizhou.com.cn/news/2018-08/05/content_6056161.htm
http://www.zjich.cn/xiangmu/xiangmushow.html?id=210
http://www.ihchina.cn/niansu/html/zhangDengJieCai_xianJuHuaDeng.html
http://www.zjich.cn/xiangmu/xiangmushow.html?id=760
https://baijiahao.baidu.com/s?id=1643081315518277656&wfr=spider&for=pc

https://www.cvtvcn.com/m/news/4c9e8cb457597c602347

http://www.xiangjianke.com/10004593.html

文化活动二：浙江油菜花节(二)

Cultural Activity (2): Zhejiang Rape Seed Flower Festival II

文化寻踪之浙里村落 Ancient Villages

➢ 仙居县高迁村

Gaoqian Village, Xianju County

高迁村位于浙江省台州市风光秀丽的仙居县白塔镇境内，毗邻国家级重点风景名胜区神仙居、景星岩。仙居山水的神奇美与高迁村的古典美得到绝妙的组合，古村的整体环境风貌基本保持完整，黑瓦、白墙、飞檐、翘角……一座座古色古香的深宅大院，让人感受到主人昔日的荣耀。古村总面积1平方公里，为省级重点文物保护单位。古村拥山环水，河流纵横，是一处融山、水、古建筑群为一体的民俗文化旅游圣地。

Gaoqian Village, which boasts a very beautiful scenery, is located in

Baita Town, Xianju County, Taizhou, Zhejiang, adjacent to the state-level key scenic spots Fairy's House and Jingxing Cliff. The classical beauty of Gaoqian Village is perfectly integrated into the marvelous beauty of Xianju's landscape, and the overall environment of the village almost remains intact: black tiles, white walls, flying eaves, rake angle, etc. When visiting these quaint houses, one can experience the glorious history of their previous owners. The village covers an area of one square kilometer, and is honourably regarded as the provincial key cultural relics protection unit. Surrounded by mountains and streams, the ancient village is really a wonderful folk cultural tourism spot with a great integreation of hills, rivers and ancient architecture.

文化寻踪之浙里印记 Cultural Imprints

建筑文化 Architectural Culture

省身堂 Xingshen Hall

省身堂反映了吴氏族人德行修炼的崇高思想境界。此堂为吴培建所建，相传其人遵循孔孟之道，恪守情操，受人敬仰。一进入省身堂，就会闻到樟木的香味，最有特色的是中堂前方屋檐下柱子上的雀替，用来支撑建筑物，使其更加稳固，体现了古代人民的智慧。

Xingshen Hall, built by Wu Peijian, reflects the lofty virtue and thoughts of Wu people. Legend has it that he was scrupulously respected for observing sentiment and following the doctrine of Confucius and Mencius. Once entering Xinshen Hall, one will smell the aroma of camphorwood. The most characteristic thing is "Que Ti" (the "carved angle brace") on the pillar of front hall. It was used to support the building and make them much stronger, which fully reflects the wisdom of ancient people.

慎德堂 Shende Hall

慎德堂是高迁村落明清住宅的精华代表作之一,也是高迁村的中心。作为耕读世家的居所,它处处充满书香气味。此堂为清代乾嘉年间吴树凤、吴熙河所造,该二人奉行以德养人、以俭治家。这里曾培养出了一名优秀士子吴蓼溪。

Shende Hall is not only one of the best works of ancient village residence of the Ming and Qing Dynasties, but also the heart of Gaoqian village. As the residece of families who laid great stress on farming and education, it is full of scholarly atmosphere. The hall was built by Wu Shufeng and Wu Xihe who advocated virtue and frugality in the Qing Dynasty. An outstanding scholar Wu Liaoxi once lived there.

➢ 非遗文化 Intangible Cultural Heritage

卵石镶嵌技艺 Pebble Inlay Technique

卵石镶嵌技艺是指利用河床的卵石,按照民俗习惯,将各式图案用镶嵌的形式铺设在墙体、天井和道路上的一种传统工艺。在高迁古宅院随处可见技艺成熟、手法独特、图案丰富和造型规范的卵石镶嵌作品。其中常见的几何图形有正方形、长方形、三角形、圆形、波浪形、菱形等，常见的图案有吉祥图案、植物图案、动物图案及图腾图案等。

Pebble inlay technique refers to a traditional craft that uses the pebbles of the river bed to lay various patterns on the walls, patios and roads in accordance with folk customs. It is widely used in the existing Gaoqian ancient buildings, and the pebble inlay works with mature skills, unique techniques, rich patterns and standardized modeling can be seen everywhere. The common geometric images of the works are square, rectangle, triangle, circle, wave, rhombus, etc. The common patterns are auspicious images, plants, animals and totems, etc.

文化寻踪之出行贴士 Travel Tips

寻踪之旅载体：浙江油菜花节(二)

寻踪之旅地点：浙江省台州市仙居县高迁村

寻踪之旅时间：通常为3月

寻踪信息查询：(1)http://www.taizhou.com.cn;(2)“仙居发布”微信公众平台;(3)搜狐、腾讯等多家网站。

Cultural Activity: Zhejiang Rape Seed Flower Festival II

Ancient Village: Gaoqian Village, Xianju County, Taizhou City, Zhejiang Province

Travel Time: Usually in March

For More Information: (1) Please visit http://www.taizhou.com.cn;

(2) Please search on the WeChat public platform "Xianju Fabu"; (3) Please visit the websites such as Sohu, Tencent, etc.

参考资料

https://baijiahao.baidu.com/s?id=1667530592062094569&wfr=spider&for=pc
https://kuaibao.qq.com/s/20200219A0IGVF00
https://www.sohu.com/a/303771479_120095517
https://www.sohu.com/a/333993345_507384
http://www.zjich.cn/zaiti/zaitishow.html?id=424
http://www.zjich.cn/xiangmu/xiangmushow.html?id=1130
http://www.rjxj.com.cn/museum/fwzwhyc/sj/lsxqjy/
http://www.ihchina.cn/Article/Index/detail?id=14213
http://blog.sina.com.cn/s/blog_603b792701013bfd.html
http://blog.sina.com.cn/s/blog_48cf452001018qo7.html
http://blog.sina.com.cn/s/blog_4cd69daf0102e9nc.html
http://www.zjww.gov.cn/news/2013-01-02/675024000.shtml
http://cxd987654321.blog.163.com/blog/static/34186265201202385351930/
http://www.people.com.cn/GB/paper447/11439/1032547.html
https://www.meipian.cn/1ykj5hz9
https://zj.zjol.com.cn/news/532470.html

文化活动三：河阳非遗文化节

Cultural Activity (3): Heyang Intangible Cultural Heritage Festival

文化寻踪之浙里村落 Ancient Villages

➢ 缙云县新建镇河阳村

Heyang Village, Xinjian Town, Jinyun County

河阳村位于浙江省丽水市缙云县新建镇镇西1.5公里，始建于五代末期，已有一千多年的历史。其距缙云县仙都国家4A级风景名胜区16公里。河阳村拥有丰富的非物质文化遗产资源，其中已列入省级非遗名录的有河阳古民居建筑艺术、缙云剪纸等。

Heyang Village is located 1.5 kilometers away from the west of Xinjian Town, Jinyun County, Lishui City, Zhejiang Province, 16 kilometers away from Xiandu National 4A Grade Scenic Spot. It was built at the end of the Five Dynasties and has a history of more than a thousand years. It is rich in intangible cultural heritages, among which Heyang Ancient Residential Architecture Art and Jinyun Paper Cutting are included in the provincial intangible heritage list.

文化寻踪之浙里印记 Cultural Imprints

建筑文化
Architectural Culture

八士门街 Bashimen Street

元代河阳最著名的建筑就是“八士门”。朱氏历代祖先以耕读传家，重农经商，人才辈出，富甲一方。宋元两代曾出八位进士，形成“义阳诗派”，相传“八士门”就是为此而建。“八士门”前还有一对无头的石狮子，石狮乃朱元璋所赠，取名“稀罕”，意指河阳一村出了八进士实属稀罕。石狮至今尚在，已有六百多年历史。“八士门”为河阳村正大门，又称为“八字门”。河阳人娶媳妇、嫁女儿、出殡都要过“八士门”，此风俗沿袭至今。

The most famous building in Heyang in the Yuan Dynasty is the “Bashimen”. The ancestors of Zhu family passed down the tradition of studying in the spare time of farming, attaching importance to agriculture and business. As a result, talented people stood out in large numbers. During the Song and Yuan Dynasties, there were eight presented scholars, forming the “Yiyang Poetry School”. Legend has it that the “Bashimen” was built for this purpose. In front of the construction is a pair of headless stone lions, gifted by Zhu Yuanzhang, an emperor of the Ming Dynasty and named “Xinhan”, which implies it is rare for such a small village to cultivate so many talents. The stone lions still exist today and have a history of more than 600 years. Being the main gate of Heyang Village, it has been a tradition for Heyang people to go through the "Bashimen" to conduct weddings or funerals.

廉让之间 Lianrangzhijian Houses

廉让之间建于清道光二十九年，是河阳所有"十八间"建筑中最精致、设施最完备的封闭形"十八间"。它有独立的自用水井，建筑分前厅、后堂、伙房、猪舍、厕所几部分，总计三十五间。外墙字画古诗保存十分完整，前厅是主人的住房，后堂为佣人住房，等级分明。中堂的横木是收租时上栏板堆谷子用的，屋背上有一石猫，为避邪所用。大门上有四个不同形状的小洞，代表月亮上下旬的变化。

Built in the 29th year of Emperor Daoguang of the Qing Dynasty, "Lianrangzhijian" houses are the most exquisite and well-equipped closed "Eighteen Rooms" among all the similar buildings in Heyang. It has independent self-use wells, and is divided into the front hall, the back hall, the kitchen, the pigsty, and the toilet, etc., totaling 35 rooms. The ancient poems, calligraphy and paintings on the outer wall are still well preserved. The front hall was the master's housing, while the back hall was the housing for servants, which manifested the distinct hierarchies. A long bar in the middle hall was used to pile up grain when collecting rent, and there was a stone cat on the roof of the house, aimed to ward off evil. There are four small holes of different shapes in the gate, representing the changes of the moon during the month.

答樵路 Daqiao Road

答樵路位于河阳村西北，是河阳的标志性建筑。此地原有答樵门，为河阳村古六门之一，取樵夫上山砍柴对答之意，所以此路叫答樵路。在答樵路上有三十二个马头状的墙头，远远望去似像是一匹匹马在仰头长啸，气势非凡。

Located in the northwest of the village, Daqiao Road is a landmark of Heyang. Originally, there stood one of the six ancient gates in the village—Daqiao Gate. The road got its name because people there would talk to the woodcutters who were on the mountain. On Daqiao Road, there are 32-horse-head walls, looking like many horses head up and howl all together.

非遗文化
Intangible Cultural Heritage

缙云剪纸 Jinyun Paper Cutting

缙云剪纸是较为古老的民间艺术，在明朝就已形成风俗。其大多以戏曲为题材，构思巧妙，制作工艺精良，具有浓郁的江南风格。其技法注重神似，以阴阳相结合，讲究大的影像轮廓，剪出影像中的细阴线，在剪人物时，不剪面部五官，主要刻画剪影动态。缙云的民间剪纸与当地民俗生活密不可分，每逢年节之期，祝寿之时，人

们都会用剪纸这种艺术形式来表达祈福迎祥的心愿。

Jinyun paper cutting is a relatively old folk art, and it became a custom in the Ming Dynasty. It is mainly based on operas, with ingenious ideas and sophisticated production techniques, presenting a strong art style of the south of the Yangtze River. The technique focuses on the spiritual conformity, and attaches importance to the large image outline. When cutting figures, the craftsman mainly cuts the silhouette dynamics rather than the facial features. Jinyun paper cutting is inseparable from the local folk life. People will use this artistic form to express their wishes for blessing and auspiciousness during the festivals and birthday celebrations.

文化寻踪之出行提示 Travel Tips

寻踪之旅载体:河阳非遗文化节

寻踪之旅地点:浙江省丽水市缙云县新建镇河阳村

寻踪之旅时间:通常为3月

寻踪信息查询:(1)http://jynews.zjol.com.cn;(2)“缙云发布”微信公众平台;(3)搜狐、腾讯等多家网站。

Cultural Activity: Heyang Intangible Cultural Heritage Festival

Ancient Village: Heyang Village, Xinjian Town, Jinyun County, Lishui City, Zhejiang Province

Travel Time: Usually in March

For More Information: (1) Please visit http://jynews.zjol.com.cn; (2) Please search on the WeChat public platform “Jinyun Fabu”; (3) Please visit the websites such as Sohu, Tencent, etc.

参考资料

http://jynews.zjol.com.cn/jynews/system/2016/09/26/020773633.shtml

http://zjnews.zjol.com.cn/system/2012/03/26/018359392.shtml

https://xw.qq.com/cmsid/20190521A0I7P200?f=dc

http://cn.chinaculture.org/portal/pubinfo/2020/07/03/200001003002001/57e5743458dc406e942e322f47ddfcbc.html

http://jynews.zjol.com.cn/jynews/system/2012/03/26/014869435.shtml

http://jynews.zjol.com.cn/jynews/system/2012/03/29/014882343.shtml

http://www. zhonghuaren. net/Index/detail/catid/2/artid/2d250e48-e1f0-43a0-ba28-b9b8176b1aae/userid/d823db48-2b78-4574-96ea-4557d9de14d7

https://www.wshgz.com/hot/299282.html

http://www.zjich.cn/xiangmu/xiangmushow.html?id=731

http://jynews.zjol.com.cn/jynews/system/2011/06/29/013929856.shtml

http://www.meifeiyi.com/news/648.html

http://jynews.zjol.com.cn/jynews/system/2008/06/16/010505894.shtml

文化活动一：畲族三月三节

Cultural Activity (1): The Traditional Festival of the She Ethnic Minority on the Third Day of the Third Lunar Month

文化活动二：乌镇香市

Cultural Activity (2): Wuzhen Incense Fair

文化活动三：三月三，踏沙滩/三月二十三开洋节

Cultural Activity (3): Having Fun on the Beach on the Third Day of the Third Lunar Month/Twenty-third of the Third Lunar Month, Beginning Celebration of Fishing Season

文化活动四：蚕花庙会

Cultural Activity (4): Silkworm Flower Temple Fair

文化活动五：龙游县的清明祭祖灯会

Cultural Activity (5): The Qingming Lantern Festival in Longyou County

文化活动六：三月三祭祖典礼

Cultural Activity (6): The Ancestor Worship Rituals on the Third Day of the Third Lunar Month

4月 April

文化活动一：畲族三月三节

Cultural Activity (1): The Traditional Festival of the She Ethnic Minority on the Third Day of the Third Lunar Month

文化寻踪之浙里村落 Ancient Towns

➢ 景宁畲族自治县鹤溪镇
Hexi Town, Jingning She Autonomous County

鹤溪镇，在浙江省丽水市景宁畲族自治县，是县政府驻地。鹤溪，古名沐鹤溪。汉初浮丘伯携双鹤隐居此间，筑台垂钓，沐鹤于溪而得名。镇辖区总面积98平方公里，人口2万，畲族人口占24%。鹤溪镇地理位置独特，民风淳朴，畲族文化底蕴深厚，古建筑极具特色，整体保护完好。2010年，鹤溪镇入第五批中国历史文化名镇。

Hexi Town, located in Jingning She Autonomous County, Lishui City, Zhejiang Province, is the seat of the county government. In the early Han Dynasty, Sr. Fu Qiu lived in seclusion here with two cranes, hence the other name of the town Muhexi, which in sound means enjoying the holiday with cranes. The town has a total area of 98 square kilometers and a population of 20,000, with the She ethnic minority accounting for 24%. Hexi Town boasts a unique geographical location, simple folk customs, profound She ethnic cultural heritage, and unique ancient buildings which are overall well preserved. In 2010, Hexi Town was selected into the fifth batch of Chinese historical and cultural towns.

文化寻踪之浙里印记 Cultural Imprints

➤ 建筑文化
Architectural Culture

景宁孔庙 Jingning Confucius Temple

景宁县孔庙是丽水市唯一保存完整的孔庙,始建于明景泰三年(1452),于2017年被省政府公布为第七批省级文物保护单位。景宁孔庙仿皇宫建筑,坐北朝南,占地面积约990.51平方米,呈对称式结构。景宁孔庙建筑规模宏大,构件精美,在500多年的历史进程中,守护着古老的畲乡文脉,对研究封建社会官宦建筑及儒家文化传承均有很高的研究价值,成为景宁文物的重要组成部分和主要标识。

First built in the third year of Emperor Jingtai's reign (1452) in the Ming Dynasty, Jingning Confucius Temple is the only well-preserved Confucius temple in Lishui City, and it was announced as the seventh batch of provincial cultural relics protection units by the provincial government in 2017. Sitting in the north and facing south, the temple is a symmetrical structure imitating the model of royal palace, and covers an area of about 990.51 square meters. With a large scale and exquisite components, the temple has a high research value for the study of the feudal society's official architecture and the inheritance of Confucius culture, which therefore has become an important cultural relic in Jingning.

➢ 非遗文化 Intangible Cultural Heritage

畲族民歌 Folk Songs of the She Ethnic Minority

畲族民歌以畲语歌唱的形式表达，以歌对话。畲族的演唱形式有独唱、对唱、齐唱等，其中无伴奏的山歌是畲族人最喜爱的一种民歌方式。畲族民歌讲究畲语押韵，不少人能即兴编唱，有的歌手甚至能对唱一两夜而不重复。畲民喜爱山歌，以歌代言，沟通感情；以歌论事，扬善惩恶；以歌传知，比睿斗智。他们不仅在婚嫁喜庆和逢年过节唱，也在生产劳动、招待客人、闲暇休息时唱。

Folk songs of the She ethnic minority are performed in the She language, and the singing forms include solo, duet, and unison, among which the unaccompanied folk song is the most favorite type by the She people. The folk songs of the She ethnic minority attach importance to the rhyming of the lyrics. Many She people can choreograph and sing improvisationally, and some may sing in antiphonal style without repeating for one or two night. The She people love folk songs and use them as their endorsements to communicate their feelings; use songs to discuss matters, promote good and punish evil; use songs to spread knowledge and compete wisdom. They not only sing on weddings and festivals, but also sing while working, entertaining guests, or in leisure time.

畲族婚俗 Marriage Customs of the She Ethnic Minority

畲族传统婚俗中，女嫁男方一般要经过相亲、定亲、送糯米等程序。婚俗彩礼包括相亲麻饼、定亲八礼及银项圈、银手镯、银戒指、衣料、酒宴糯米、若干红包等。婚礼的特色较多。迎亲队伍到村时，嫁方村上女性拿杉木枝拦路，表示晚上要对歌；中餐由嫁方请迎亲队伍，媒人就座中堂席首位，叫“落脚酒”；晚餐由娶方请嫁方亲戚朋友，舅公就座首席，叫“请大酒”。

In the traditional marriage custom of the She ethnic minority, it usually goes through procedures such as blind date, engagement, giving glutinous rice, etc. The traditional betrothal gifts include sesame pancake for the dating, eight engagement gifts and silver necklace, silver bracelets, silver rings, clothing materials, glutinous rice for banquets, some red gift money, etc. The She wedding has many features. When the team to fetch the bride arrive in the village, women in the bride's village will take the cedar branches, which is a signal of competing singing in antiphonal style at night; the bridegroom's family and friends will be invited for lunch hosted by the bride's side, with the matchmaker sitting in the center of the hall; while for dinner, the bride's family and friends will be treated by the bridegroom's side, with the granduncle sitting in the center.

景宁畲族祭祀仪式 Sacrificial Rituals of the She Ethnic Minority in Jingning

畲族祭祀仪式是畲族民间习俗的重要组成部分，特点鲜明，其中所蕴含的民俗礼仪、舞蹈动作、演唱音调等都不同程度地印证了景宁畲族先民开创时期进行刀耕火种的农耕文明和生态环境。其具代表性的仪式有传师学师和做功德。传师学师是畲族祭祀祖先的典礼，又称“做阳”。做功德是畲族人在成年人死后，家属为“超度亡灵”而举行的传统祭祀仪式，也称“做阴”。

She sacrificial rituals are an important part of the She's folk custom, full of distinctive characteristics. The folk etiquettes, dance movements, singing tones, and the like demonstrate the slash-and-burn farming civilization and the ecological environment of the pioneering period. The representative rituals include “Zuoyang” and “Zuoyin”. “Zuoyang” is a ceremony for the She people to worship their ancestors, while “Zuoyin” is a traditional sacrificial ceremony held by the family members to “release souls from purgatory” after the death of an adult.

畲族三月三 The Traditional Festival of the She People on the Third Day of the Third Lunar Month

三月初三是畲族的传统节日，畲族三月三节是景宁最盛大的民间传统节日，是景宁畲族人民悼念勤劳勇敢的祖先、表达对爱情和幸福向往之情的传统节日。每年这一天人们祭祀祖先拜谷神，而且举行盛大的歌会，载歌载舞。他们还会采摘乌稔树叶，用嫩叶的汁液浸泡糯米蒸制成乌米饭，款待来客，以驱邪祈福，因此畲族三月三又称“乌饭节”。畲族三月三

节所呈现出的各种习俗包含了民族音乐、服饰、体育以及人际交往等样式，涉及生活的各个方面，具有鲜明的民族特征和浓郁的乡土气息。

The third day of March in the lunar calendar is a traditional festival of the She people. It is the grandest folk traditional festival in Jingning, when the She people mourn their hard-working and brave ancestors and express their yearning for love and happiness. On this day of the year, people worship their ancestors and the gods of grain, while holding a grand party to sing and dance. Picking leaves of oriental blueberry, soaking glutinous rice in the juice of the tender leaves, and steaming the rice, the She people entertain guests with their specialty, namely Wumifan (black rice), on the particular day, meaning driving out evil spirits and praying for blessings. Therefore, the festival is also called "Black Rice Festival". The various customs presented on the festival include cultural styles such as folk music, costumes, sports, and interpersonal communication, involving all aspects of life, with distinctive ethnic characteristics and a strong local flavor.

文化寻踪之出行贴士 Travel Tips

寻踪之旅载体：畲族三月三节

寻踪之旅地点：浙江省丽水市景宁畲族自治县鹤溪镇

寻踪之旅时间：通常为4月

寻踪信息查询：（1）http://www.jingning.gov.cn；（2）"景宁文旅"微信公

众平台;(3)搜狐、腾讯等多家网站。

Cultural Activity: The Traditional Festival of the She Ethnic Minority on the Third Day of the Third Lunar Month

Ancient Town: Hexi Town, Jingning She Autonomous County, Lishui City, Zhejiang Province

Travel Time: Usually in April

For More Information: (1) Please visit http://www.jingning.gov.cn; (2) Please search on the WeChat public platform "Jingning Wenlv"; (3) Please visit the websites such as Sohu, Tencent, etc.

参考资料

https://www.douban.com/note/725370978/

http://www.jingning.gov.cn/col/col1376105/index.html

http://www.jingning.gov.cn/art/2018/12/14/art_1376115_27368989.html

http://jnnews.zjol.com.cn/jnnews/system/2010/04/19/012034832.shtml

http://www.jingning.gov.cn/art/2019/10/12/art_1229441360_2113973.html

http://www.huaxia.com/ly/lyzx/2014/04/3829577.html

https://xw.qq.com/cmsid/20200602A0GFUE00?f=newdc

https://www.meipian.cn/445kzu8

http://www.zjich.cn/xiangmu/xiangmushow.html?id=363

http://www.zjich.cn/xiangmu/xiangmushow.html?id=1740

http://www.zjich.cn/xiangmu/xiangmushow.html?id=563

https://www.sohu.com/a/250580651_155927

https://www.sohu.com/a/331453975_653481

http://www.zjich.cn/xiangmu/xiangmushow.html?id=321

https://www.sohu.com/a/130853814_531786

https://baijiahao.baidu.com/s?id=1688359620025032423&wfr=spider&for=pc

https://m.gmw.cn/baijia/2021-01/09/1302016906.html

http://news.ifeng.com/c/7fbkoyNRhQ6

文化活动二:乌镇香市

Cultural Activity (2): Wuzhen Incense Fair

文化寻踪之浙里村落 Ancient Towns

➢ 桐乡市乌镇

Wuzhen Town, Tongxiang City

乌镇在浙江省桐乡市,是江南水乡六大古镇之一,是中国现代文学巨匠茅盾的出生地。乌镇是首批中国历史文化名镇、中国十大魅力名镇、全国环境优美乡镇、国家5A级景区,素有“中国最后的枕水人家”之誉。乌镇是典型的中国江南水乡古镇,享有“鱼米之乡、丝绸之府”之称。

Wuzhen is one of the six ancient towns in the south of the Yangtze River in Tongxiang City, Zhejiang Province. It is the birthplace of Mao Dun, who is a legend of modern Chinese literature. Wuzhen is listed on the first batch of Chinese historical and cultural towns, China's top ten charming towns, China's beautiful towns and a national 5A-level scenic spot. It is known as "the last riverside hometown in China". It is a typical ancient water town in the south of the Yangtze River in China, and is reputed as the "land of fish and rice and the home of silk".

文化寻踪之浙里印记 Cultural Imprints

➢ 非遗文化 Intangible Cultural Heritage

乌镇竹编 Wuzhen Bamboo Weaving

竹编是以竹子为原材料，经过纯手工编织的手法，制成许多生产、生活和观赏性的竹制品。乌镇竹编始于唐朝，盛于明清，竹编的编制方式大致可以分为交叉、人字、方格、六角等120多种。多种编织手法的灵活运用，可以形成形态各异、功能不同的竹制品。

Bamboo weaving takes bamboo as the raw material, through pure hand weaving techniques, to make many production, life and ornamental bamboo products. Wuzhen bamboo weaving began in the Tang Dynasty and flourished in the Ming and Qing Dynasties. The weaving methods can be roughly divided into more than 120 types such as cross, herringbone, square, hexagon, etc. The flexible use of a variety of weaving techniques can form bamboo products with different shapes and functions.

乌镇香市 Wuzhen Incense Fair

乌镇香市是江南一带特有的民间民俗活动，即历年清明至谷雨时分，江南百姓为祈求蚕桑丰收而烧香祈福，当地百姓广为参与，各路戏班、杂耍齐来助兴的一个民间民俗的狂欢节。香市这一民间风俗在乌镇流传已久，被茅盾先生称为“中国农村的狂欢节”。

Wuzhen Incense Fair is a local folklore activity unique to the south region of the Yangtze River in China, spanning from the period of Qingming to Grain Rain every year. The local people prayed for a good sericulture harvest and burned incense to pray for blessings. The local people participated widely, and various theatrical troupes and vaudevilles came together to entertain. The folk custom of incense fair has been prevailing in Wuzhen for a long time, and Mr. Mao Dun called it “the carnival in rural China”.

乌镇水阁 Wuzhen Waterside Pavilion

乌镇古民居属典型的江南水乡建筑艺术，其中以水阁最为常见。水阁是乌镇独具一格的建筑形式，其构造为在傍河的房屋背后，利用木桩或石柱打入河床，上架横梁，搁上木板，悬空建房于河面。水阁具有三面临河、空气流通、阳光充足的特点，人居其间，凭窗眺望，水上风光一览无遗。水阁建筑在乌镇河流沿岸随处可见，东栅、西栅、南

栅、北栅都有，其中以西栅最为壮观，连绵蜿蜒1.8公里。

The ancient dwellings in Wuzhen are of typical water town architectural style, among which waterside pavilion (the buildings on the river) are the most classic ones. Waterside pavilion is a unique architectural form in Wuzhen. Behind the houses near the river, wooden piles or stone pillars were drived into the riverbed, with the beams and planks constructed above, so the houses suspended on the river surface. Such buildings have the characteristics of facing the river from three sides, good air circulation, and plenty of sunshine. Looking out from the window of waterside pavilion, the scenery on the water is unobstructed. Waterside pavilion can be seen everywhere along the rivers in Wuzhen, including Dongzha, Xizha, Nanzha, and Beizha. Among them, Xizha is the most spectacular one, with a total length of 1.8 kilometers.

乌镇蚕桑习俗 Sericulture Custom

乌镇的蚕农们为了祈求风调雨顺、蚕桑丰收会举行一项十分古老的蚕事风俗活动。据桐乡方志，乌镇的蚕桑习俗距今已有一百多年的历史。所谓“蚕花”，就是用五颜六色的绉纸扎成的纸花。“轧”是方言词，挤的意思。传说蚕花娘娘在清明节化作村姑，踏遍含山，在山上留下“蚕气”。谁能到含山踏青，谁就能把蚕花喜气带回家，得到蚕花“廿四分”（即双倍丰收之意）。所以，每年清明节，八方蚕农争相上含山。长期以来，蚕桑习俗已经融入了桐乡老百姓的衣食住行、婚丧嫁娶之中，一些由蚕而起的传统习俗一直保留至今。

The custom of sericulture in Wuzhen is a very ancient activity held by silkworm raisers in order to pray for good weather and a good harvest.

According to the records of Tongxiang local chronicles, it has a history of more than one hundred years. The so-called "silkworm flowers" are paper flowers tied with colorful crepe paper. "Ga" ("轧") means "squeeze" ("挤"), which are the same in dialect sound. Legend has it that the silkworm flower empress turned into a village girl during the Qingming Festival and walked all over Mount Hanshan, leaving "silkworm energy" on the mountain. Anyone who can go to Mount Hanshan for an outing can bring the silkworm luck home with joy, and get double harvest. Therefore, every year on the Qingming festival, silkworm raisers from all directions flood to Mount Hanshan. For a long time, the sericulture custom has been integrated into the dieting, clothing, housing, transportation, weddings and funerals of the local people, and some has been preserved to this day.

蓝印花布印染技艺 Blue Calico Printing and Dyeing Technique

蓝印花布,在中国民间艺术中堪称独树一帜,距今已有1300多年的历史,是江南水乡一带的传统服饰织品,在桐乡还被广泛用在被面、蚊帐、包袱等上。蓝印花布印染技艺是利用物理防染印花法在自然白色坯布上隔染而成的民间染整技艺。据有关记载,清末民初桐乡共开办印染作坊数十家之多,其中较有名的是丰子恺的祖父丰小康在1841年创办的石门丰同裕和崇福蓝家创办于清光绪年间的蓝茂丰等染坊。蓝印花布整个印染工艺流程全部采用手工操作,图案题材十分丰富,排列自由多变,具有极为鲜明的江南风格。

The blue calico, with a history of over 1,300 years, is unique among the Chinese folk art. It is a traditional apparel fabric in the water towns of the south of the Yangtze River, widely used in quilts, mosquito nets, and bags, etc., in Tongxiang. The blue calico printing and dyeing technique is a folk craft that uses a physical anti-dye printing method to separate the natural white fabric from dyeing. According to relevant records, dozens of printing and dyeing workshops were established in Tongxiang in the years of the late Qing Dynasty and the early Republic of China, among which the most famous ones were the Fengtongyu and Lanmaofeng respectively founded by Feng Zikai's (the pioneer of modern Chinese comics) grandfather in 1841 and Lan family in the reign of Emperor Guangxu in the Qing Dynasty. The entire printing and dyeing process of the blue calico is all manually operated. With rich pattern themes and flexible arrangements, it has a very distinctive art style of the south of the Yangtze River.

文化寻踪之出行贴士 Travel Tips

寻踪之旅载体:乌镇香市

寻踪之旅地点:浙江省桐乡市乌镇

寻踪之旅时间:通常为4月

寻踪信息查询:(1)http://www.wuzhen.com.cn/;(2)"乌镇景区"微信公众平台;(3)搜狐、腾讯等多家网站。

Cultural Activity: Wuzhen Incense Fair

Ancient Town: Wuzhen Town, Tongxiang City, Zhejiang Province

Travel Time: Usually in April

For More Information: (1) Please visit http://www.wuzhen.com.cn/; (2) Please search on the WeChat public platform "Wuzhen Jingqu"; (3) Please visit the websites such as Sohu, Tencent, etc.

参考资料

https://www.sohu.com/a/147707375_489901

https://www.sohu.com/a/386785873_396008

http://www.zjich.cn/xiangmu/xiangmushow.html?id=2282

https://www.163.com/dy/article/G4CKS7810517M96Q.html

http://www.zjich.cn/xiangmu/xiangmushow.html?id=1475

http://www.wuzhen.com.cn/web/folk/details?id=2

https://www.sohu.com/a/321292476_100014684

http://www.zjich.cn/xiangmu/xiangmushow.html?id=870

https://www.sohu.com/a/403605554_120056046

http://www.chinadaily.com.cn/travel/2014-07/23/content_17908970.htm

http://www.zjich.cn/xiangmu/xiangmushow.html?id=296

http://cxnews.zjol.com.cn/cxnews/system/2009/12/09/011653172.shtml

http://www.jiaxing.gov.cn/art/2014/1/13/art_1536221_22023146.html

http://www.ihchina.cn/project_details/15232/

https://www.ciae.com.cn/detail/zh/36283.html

http://www.zjich.cn/xiangmu/xiangmushow.html?id=1744

https://zjnews. zjol. com. cn/zjnews/hznews/201907/t20190704_10517154. shtml

文化活动三：三月三，踏沙滩/三月二十三开洋节

Cultural Activity (3): Having Fun on the Beach on the Third Day of the Third Lunar Month/Twenty-Third of the Third Lunar Month, Beginning Celebration of Fishing Season

文化寻踪之浙里村落 Ancient Towns

➢ 象山县石浦镇

Shipu Town, Xiangshan County

石浦镇位于浙江沿海中部，现为全国六大中心渔港之一，是唯一临港型中国历史文化名镇，唯一以海洋渔文化为特色的国家级生态保护实验区核心区，被誉为“活着的渔文化博物馆”。几千年的历史发展为石浦沉淀下了宝贵的渔文化、海商文化、海防文化、饮食文化等海洋文化遗产。

Shipu Town is situated in the middle of Zhejiang's coast. It is now one of the six major central fishing ports in the country, and the only port-type Chinese historical and cultural town, as well as the core area of the national ecological protection experimental area featuring marine fishing culture. With thousands of years of historical development, the town is reputed as the "live museum of fishery culture", and boasts precious marine cultural heritage such as fishing culture, maritime business culture, coastal defense culture, and food culture.

文化寻踪之浙里印记 Cultural Imprints

非遗文化
Intangible Cultural Heritage

开洋节/谢洋节 Beginning/Thanksgiving Celebration of Fishing Season

象山开洋节、谢洋节包括渔民祭祀活动和传统民间文艺表演等内容，距今已有一千多年的历史。开洋节是渔船出海时，渔民祈求平安、丰收的民俗活动。谢洋节则是渔船出海平安归来，渔民为了感恩大海的民俗活动。这些活动的原始意义是希望神灵保佑出海能一帆风顺、满载而归。祭海神酒又分为开洋酒和谢洋酒。每逢春汛、夏汛、秋汛和冬汛的第一天出海之前，渔家总要聚集港湾滩头，举行祭海神仪式。仪式结束后，渔民就在海滩上大碗大碗地饮酒，以壮开洋征海之行色，以求一汛之丰收，此为开洋酒。谢洋酒，则是渔民为庆贺一个鱼汛的丰收，也为感谢海神的护佑，在海滩举行的祭海仪式。

The festivals to celebrate the beginning and ending of fishing season in Xiangshan have a history of more than a thousand years, and the activities on the festivals include fishermen's sacrificial rituals and traditional folk performances. The beginning celebration of fishing season is a folk event where fishermen pray for safety and a good harvest when fishing boats go out to sea. The thanksgiving celebration of fishing season is a folklore activity for fishingmen to extend their thanks to the sea. The two activities are to pray for a smooth fishing journey and a good harvest. Offering sacrifices basically wine to the sea god is a traditional custom for Shipu's fishermen, which usually includes opening wine and thanksgiving wine. On the first day of spring, summer, autumn and winter fishing seasons, fishermen gather at the port to offer sacrifices to the sea god praying for a harvest. After the ceremony, the fishermen will drink with big bowls on the beach so as to boost the morale and pray for a good season. This is called opening wine. While the thanksgiving wine is a ceremony held after the fishing season with the aim to celebrate the bumper harvest and express their gratitude to the protection of the sea god.

象山渔民号子 Xiangshan Fishermen's Songs

象山渔民号子，由传统渔业生产中的渔民号子和海洋运输业中的船工号子等组成。它是渔民、船工在长期的生产、劳动实践中自发创造的一种文化现象。它有着与众不同的独特风格和强烈的海洋生活气息，充满着渔民（船工）的乐观主义精神和雄壮、豪迈、朴实、奔放的个性。石浦、爵溪是象山渔民号子的主要发源地和传承地。象山渔民号子在唐宋时期已经初步形成，清康熙年间至民国期间达到繁荣。象山渔民号子品种相对较全，曲调粗犷优美，有着鲜明的海洋文化特征，具有厚重的历史价值和独特的艺术价值。

Xiangshan fishermen's songs are composed of fishermen's chants in the traditional fishery production and boatmen's chants in the marine transportation. It is a cultural phenomenon spontaneously created by fishermen and boatmen in their long-term production and labor practices. It has a distinctive and unique style and a strong atmosphere of marine life, full of the optimistic spirit of fishermen and boatmen, and a majestic, heroic, simple and unrestrained personality. Shipu and Juexi are the main origins and inheritance places of Xiangshan fishermen's songs. Initially formed during the Tang and Song Dynasties, flourished during the Kangxi period of the Qing Dynasty and the Republic of China, Xiangshan fishermen's songs are relatively complete in variety, rough and beautiful in tunes, and have a heavy historical value and a unique artistic value.

文化寻踪之出行贴士 Travel Tips

寻踪之旅载体:三月三,踏沙滩/三月二十三开洋节

寻踪之旅地点:浙江省宁波市象山县石浦镇

寻踪之旅时间:通常为4月

寻踪信息查询:(1)http://www.xiangshan.gov.cn;(2)"石浦发布"微信公众平台;(3)搜狐、腾讯等多家网站。

Cultural Activity: Having Fun on the Beach on the Third Day of the Third Lunar Month/Twenty-Third of the Third Lunar Month, Beginning Celebration of Fishing Season

Ancient Town: Shipu Town, Xiangshan County, Ningbo City, Zhejiang Province

Travel Time: Usually in April

For More Information: (1) Please visit http://www.xiangshan.gov.cn; (2) Please search on the WeChat public platform "Shipu Fabu"; (3) Please visit the websites such as Sohu, Tencent, etc.

参考资料

https://www.sohu.com/a/137089455_525464
http://www.zjich.cn/xiangmu/xiangmushow.html?id=282
http://yynews.cnnb.com.cn/system/2017/05/04/011554476.shtml
http://www.zjich.cn/xiangmu/xiangmushow.html?id=283
http://www.ihchina.cn/project_details/15145/
https://www.sohu.com/a/335078575_781189
http://www.zjich.cn/xiangmu/xiangmushow.html?id=408
https://www.sohu.com/a/147250285_781189
https://www.sohu.com/a/329038720_100020365
http://www.ihchina.cn/Article/Index/detail?id=12631
http://www.xiangshan.gov.cn/art/2019/9/6/art_1229045037_44423796.html
http://nbxssp.zjzwfw.gov.cn/col/col1047426/index.html
http://zt.cnnb.com.cn/system/2015/02/27/008269894.shtml
https://www.sohu.com/a/130574125_160869
https://xw.qq.com/cmsid/20200326A08ZRH00
http://www.nbwb.net/pd_xsyj/info.aspx?Id=26842

文化活动四:蚕花庙会

Cultural Activity (4): Silkworm Flower Temple Fair

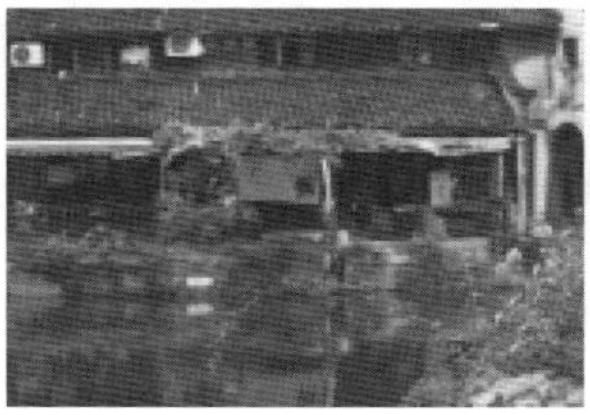

文化寻踪之浙里村落 Ancient Towns

➢ 德清县新市镇

Xinshi Town, Deqing County

新市镇始建于西晋永嘉年间,已有1700多年的历史,自古以来便是浙北地区的商贸重镇和文化名镇。新市镇商贸活跃,依托京杭大运河水道的交通便利,成为重要的丝绸、茶叶、大米等商品的集散地。新市镇拥有别具一格的民俗文化和商贸文化,是中国古代丝绸之路的发源地之一。

Xinshi Town was built in the reign of Emperor Yongjia of the Western Jin Dynasty and has a history of more than 1,700 years. Since ancient times, it has been an important commercial and cultural town in northern Zhejiang. Xinshi Town has been active in commerce and trade.

Relying on the convenient transportation of the Beijing-Hangzhou Grand Canal, it has become an important distribution center for silk, tea, rice and other commodities. The folk culture and business culture of the town are rich and unique. Xinshi Town is one of the birthplaces of the ancient Silk Road in China.

文化寻踪之浙里印记 Cultural Imprints

➢ 建筑文化 Architectural Culture

新市河埠群 Xinshi Ferry Group

新市河埠群位于新市镇西河口到陈家潭一线的河流西岸,由驳岸和河埠组成。驳岸长约1100米,出水高约2米,均由条石砌筑,其用材也多选用本地特有的武康石。驳岸上嵌有各种造型的缆船石和下水口近150个,缆船石种类齐全;下水口造型各异,极富特色。河埠共34处,造型多变。新市河埠群遗存丰富、类型多样、特色明显,在充分展示水乡风貌的同时,也凸显了建筑价值与运河文化。

Xinshi ferry group is located on the west bank of the river along the west river mouth to the Chenjia Pond, and consists of the revetment and river ports. The revetment is about 1,100 meters long, and the water outlet is about 2 meters high. They are all made of striped stones, and the materials used are mostly local unique Wukang stones. There are nearly 150 cable boat rocks and water outlets of various shapes embedded on the barge. The cable boat rocks are diversified, while the water outlets are different and distinctive. There are a total of 34 river ports, with various designs. The ferry group of Xinshi has rich relics, diverse types and obvious characteristics. It reflects the condition and intensity of water conservancy traffic in canal towns. While fully demonstrating the style of the water town, the ferry group also highlights the architectural value and canal culture.

南圣堂 Nansheng Hall

南圣堂，位于新市南昌街中段，砖木结构建筑，硬山顶，建筑面积28平方米，为历代运河渔民祭祀场所，是运河古迹。始建于清代康熙年间，在咸丰元年、1923年以及2007年均有重修。

Nansheng Hall, located in the middle section of Nanchang Street, Xinshi, is a brick-wood structure building with a flush gable roof and a building area of 28 square meters. It is a worship place for fishermen from the canal in the past. First built in the reign of Emperor Kangxi of the Qing Dynasty, it was rebuilt respectively in the first year of Emperor Xianfeng, 1923 and 2007.

刘王庙戏台题记 Liuwang Temple Stage Inscription

刘王庙，位于新市朱家桥刘王堂弄，始建于南宋，是德清县现存较为完整的古建筑之一。该庙坐北朝南，砖木结构，石库大门坐西朝东，总占地面积600平方米，现存石刻大门、戏台及大殿。大门是清代乾隆年间所重建。2007年，当地政府在修复刘王庙古戏台时，发现了一面墙壁上有100多年前的珍贵戏曲墨记，上面记载着清代同治至光绪年间到刘王庙戏台演出的戏班名和所演剧目名。

Liuwang Temple, located in Liuwang Alley, Zhujiaqiao, Xinshi, was built in the Southern Song Dynasty. It is one of the relatively complete surviving ancient structures in Deqing County. The temple faces south from the north and has a brick-wood structure. With an area of 600 square meters, the temple retains structures including stone carved gates, stage and main hall. The gate was rebuilt during the reign of Emperor Qianlong of the Qing Dynasty. In 2007, when the local government was restoring the ancient stage of Liuwang Temple, they found a wall with precious ink notes of operas more than 100 years ago, which recorded the names of the troupes and the repertoire performed on the stage from the years of Emperor Tongzhi to Guangxu in the Qing Dynasty.

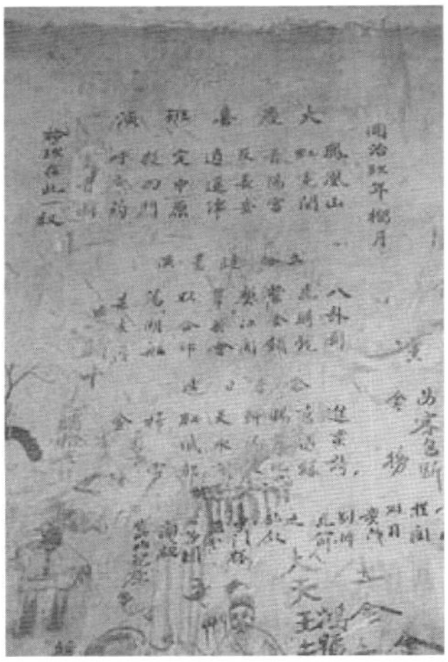

非遗文化
Intangible Cultural Heritage

新市蚕花庙会 Xinshi Silkworm Flower Temple Fair

新市建镇已有1700多年的历史，养蚕缫丝自古就是当地农民的经济来源，然而蚕宝宝向来娇贵难养，为了每年的收成好，蚕农们总要在养蚕季节到来之前，祈神拜天一番。久而久之，清明节就成了约定俗成的蚕花庙会。传统庙会自三月起至四月二十日止，主要内容有踏青、花灯、祭蚕神、拈香、请神出游、划龙舟、打拳船、请蚕花、轧蚕花、演蚕花戏、商贸集市等。新市蚕花庙会历史悠久，延续时间长，规模庞大，是杭嘉湖地区最为盛大的蚕桑和清明节庆民俗之一。

Xinshi has been set as a town for more than 1,700 years. Sericulture and silk reeling have been the main source of income for local farmers since ancient times. However, it has been a tough and delicate job to raise silkworms, therefore, the silkworm raisers used to worship the goddess in the hope of a good harvest before sericulture season arrived. Over time, the Qingming festival has become a customary silkworm flower temple fair, which starts from March to April 20th in accordance with the lunar calendar. The main activities include going hiking on a spring day, enjoying lanterns, offering sacrifices to the silkworm goddess, etc. Boasting a long history, a long duration, and a large scale, Xinshi Silkworm Flower Temple Fair is one of the grandest sericulture and Qingming festival folk customs in Hangzhou-Jiaxing-Huzhou area.

文化寻踪之出行贴士 Travel Tips

寻踪之旅载体:蚕花庙会

寻踪之旅地点:浙江省湖州市德清县新市镇

寻踪之旅时间:通常为4月

寻踪信息查询:(1)http://www.deqing.gov.cn;(2)“德清新市发布”微信公众平台;(3)搜狐、腾讯等多家网站。

Cultural Activity: Silkworm Flower Temple Fair

Ancient Town: Xinshi Town, Deqing County, Huzhou City, Zhejiang Province

Travel Time: Usually in April

For More Information: (1) Please visit http://www.deqing.gov.cn; (2) Please search on the WeChat public platform “Deqing Xinshi Fabu”; (3) Please visit the websites such as Sohu, Tencent, etc.

参考资料

http://www.xinhuanet.com/world/2015-06/21/c_127936595_3.htm

http://huzdqxs.zjzwfw.gov.cn/col/col913612/index.html

https://baijiahao.baidu.com/s?id=1638180957617008248&wfr=spider&for=pc

http://www.xinhuanet.com/2019-07/05/c_1210181293.htm

http://blog.sina.com.cn/s/blog_7b86ff370101by45.html

http://blog.sina.com.cn/s/blog_49b6be160102yabj.html

http://wwj.zj.gov.cn/art/2011/7/29/art_1228971631_40465429.html

http://www.deqing.gov.cn/hzgov/front/s134/lhjs/cgtgzs/ggwhfw/ggfw/wbdwml/20201208/i2854971.html

https://m.hk.guom.site/zh-sg/%E5%88%98%E7%8E%8B%E5%BA%99

http://www.zjich.cn/xiangmu/xiangmushow.html?id=839

https://www.sohu.com/a/227363010_366205

http://www.zjdfz.cn/html/2014/msfw_0304/2312.html

https://zj.zjol.com.cn/red_boat.html?id=100700767

http://cs.zjol.com.cn/kzl/202104/t20210406_22348681.shtml

文化活动五:龙游县的清明祭祖灯会

Cultural Activity (5):

The Qingming Lantern Festival in Longyou County

文化寻踪之浙里村落 Ancient Villages

➢ 龙游县石佛乡三门源村

Sanmenyuan Village, Shifo Town, Longyou County

三门源村位于龙游县北部,距离县城26公里。由于进出须经三道屏障,又有一条碧溪穿村而过,故称"三门源"。三门源村主要有叶、翁两大姓氏,其中翁氏于北宋末年避战乱迁居至此事农耕,叶氏于南宋咸淳六年(1270)迁居筑室务商业,两姓人隔碧溪对峙融合,形成独特的历史传承格局。

Sanmenyuan Village is located in the north of Longyou County, 26 kilometers away from the county seat. Since there are three barriers to enter and exit, and there is the Bixi Stream running through the village, it is called "Sanmenyuan" (three gates and a stream). Sanmenyuan Village mainly has two large families, i. e. Family Ye and Family Weng. The Weng family escaped from the war in the late Northern Song Dynasty and moved here for farming. The Ye family moved to construct buildings and do business in the sixth year of the reign of Emperor Xianchun (1270) in the Southern Song Dynasty. The two families have lived opposite the stream, forming a unique historical residence pattern.

文化寻踪之浙里印记 Cultural Imprints

建筑文化 Architectural Culture

叶氏建筑群(艺术砖雕)Ye's Residential Complex (Art Brick Carving)

三门源村现存明清建筑50余幢,建筑沿三门源溪两岸依山势而筑,其中以2013年被公布为国家重点文物保护单位的叶氏民居建筑群最为豪华精致。叶氏民居现存3幢,有江南地区保存最为完整的、罕见的砖雕门楼。江南徽派建筑的门楼砖雕常以亭台楼阁、博古花鸟、古树名木、渔樵耕读人物为主,而叶氏民居现存的3座门楼上,主角却是婺剧剧目中的人物。3座门楼上的砖雕每块长56厘米、宽26厘米,共展现了23出婺剧曲目。三门源村叶氏民居距今已有170多年的历史,门楼上的这些工艺精湛且保存完整的浮雕造型栩栩如生,可以说是戏曲活化石。

There are currently more than 50 Ming and Qing buildings in Sanmenyuan Village. The buildings were built along the banks of the stream at the foot of the mountains, among which, the Ye's residential complex, which was announced as a national key cultural relic protection unit in 2013, is the most luxurious and exquisite. The existing three residences of the Ye family retain the most intact and rare brick-carved gatehouses in the south of the Yangtze River. The gatehouse brick carvings of Huizhou-style architecture often feature pavilions, flowers and birds, trees, fishermen, farmers, etc., while those on the Ye's residential complex depict the characters in the repertoire of Wu Opera. Each of the brick carvings on the three gatehouses is 56 cm long and 26 cm wide, presenting a total of 23 Wu Opera repertoires. The residences of the Ye family in Sanmenyuan Village have a history of more than 170 years, but the brick carvings on the gatehouses are still exquisite and well-preserved, which can be seen as the living fossils of opera.

➢ 非遗文化
Intangible Cultural Heritage

龙游皮纸制作技艺 Longyou Leather Paper Making Skills

流传于浙江龙游的皮纸制作技艺已有1400多年的历史。主要制作原料为三桠皮、雁皮和青檀皮，制作工艺分皮料制作和成品制成2个流程30多道工序，有30多个皮纸品种，不仅用于书画，还用于装帧、包装等。龙游皮纸制作过程全凭手工艺人的肉眼观察和手感经验把握，每道工序全凭手工完成。

The leather paper making skills passed down in Longyou, Zhejiang Province have a history of more than 1,400 years. The main raw materials for the production are mitsumata, gampi and wingceltis. The production is divided into two processes—leather production and finished product production, with more than 30 procedures. There are more than 30 varieties of leather paper, which can be used not only for painting and calligraphy, but also for binding and packaging. The production process of Longyou leather paper is completely based on the naked eye observation and hand feeling experience of the craftsmen. Each process is completed by hand.

龙游婺剧 Longyou Wu Opera

龙游婺剧是流传于龙游、金华、衢州一带的高腔、昆曲、乱弹、徽戏、滩簧、时调六大剧种的总称，其统一风格主要依靠金华、衢州、龙游等方言的表演语言以及器乐和锣鼓点子来形成，至今有400多年的历史。据《龙游县志》，龙游婺剧和戏曲家李渔、洪昇等人的活动有紧密的联系，历史上涌现出了周越先、周越桂、徐汝英等一批婺剧名家，有"东看西看还看龙游花旦"的美称。

Longyou Wu Opera is a general term for the six major opera types of Gaoqiang, Kunqu Opera, Luantan, Hui Opera, Tanhuang, and Shi Tune that were popular in Longyou, Jinhua, and Quzhou. Its unified style mainly relies on the performance language of dialects such as Jinhua, Quzhou, and Longyou, and is accompanied by the instrumental music, and gongs and drums, boasting a history of more than 400 years. According to *Longyou County Chronicles*, Longyou Wu Opera was closely related to the activities of opera artists Li Yu, Hong Sheng, etc. In history, a group of famous Wu Opera artists such as Zhou Yuexian, Zhou Yuegui and Xu Ruying have emerged, "Longyou Huadan (female role)" has been well known in the opera circle.

龙游发糕制作 Longyou Steamed Sponge Cake

据《龙游县志》,龙游发糕的制作始于明初,距今已有600多年的历史。据说清代乾隆皇帝游江南时品尝过龙游发糕,并对发糕的色、香、味、形大加赞赏。之后,龙游发糕一直作为贡品,进贡朝廷。龙游发糕是用上等粳米为主料,以白糖、猪油、蜜枣等为配料,按自然发酵蒸制而成的名点。龙游发糕制作工艺独特,配料考究,成品色泽洁白如玉,孔细似针,闻之鲜香扑鼻,食之甜而不腻、糯而不黏,堪称江南一绝。因"发糕"为"福高"之谐音,寓"年年发、步步高"之吉祥含义,故发糕既为逢年过节必备名点,又是馈赠亲友之佳品。

According to *Longyou County Chronicles*, the production of Longyou steamed sponge cake began in the early Ming Dynasty and has a long history of more than 600 years. It is said that Emperor Qianlong of the Qing Dynasty greatly admired the color, fragrance, taste and shape of the Longyou steamed sponge cake when he traveled to the south of the Yangtze River. After that, it had been used as a tribute to the court for many years. Longyou steamed sponge cake is made by natural fermentation and steamed with top-quality rice as the main ingredient, adding white sugar, lard, candied dates, etc. With unique craftsmanship and sophisticated ingredients, the cake is regarded as a top delicacy in the south of the Yangtze River. This is because the steamed sponge cake ("fa gao" in sound) is a homophonic of "Fu Gao", which means abundant luck, and embodies the auspicious meaning of "making a big fortune and developing year by year". It is not only a must-have food for festivals, but also an excellent gift for relatives and friends.

文化寻踪之出行贴士 Travel Tips

寻踪之旅载体:龙游县的清明祭祖灯会

寻踪之旅地点:浙江省衢州市龙游县石佛乡三门源村

寻踪之旅时间:通常为4月,隔年进行一次

寻踪信息查询:(1)http://www.longyou.gov.cn/;(2)“文旅龙游”微信公众平台;(3)搜狐、腾讯等多家网站。

Cultural Activity: The Qingming Lantern Festival in Longyou County

Ancient Village: Sanmenyuan Village, Shifo Town, Longyou County, Quzhou City, Zhejiang Province

Travel Time: Usually in April, held every two years

For More Information: (1) Please visit http://www.longyou.gov.cn/; (2) Please search on the WeChat public platform “Wenlv Longyou”; (3) Please visit the websites such as Sohu, Tencent, etc.

参考资料

https://kuaibao.qq.com/s/20191116A03NZE00
https://baijiahao.baidu.com/s?id=1669975740935956583&wfr=spider&for=pc
https://www.sohu.com/a/128213923_525464
https://www.xuexi.cn/9019ac99baeffcb01a98d74624bb9e07/e43e220633a65f9b6d8b53712cba9caa.html
http://www.zjich.cn/xiangmu/xiangmushow.html?id=1380
http://www.zjich.cn/xiangmu/xiangmushow.html?id=419

http://www.ihchina.cn/Article/Index/detail?id=14381

http://www.zjda.gov.cn/art/2018/9/14/art_1500203_21203147.html

http://khnews.zjol.com.cn/khnews/system/2019/07/01/031748890.shtml

http://www.zjich.cn/xiangmu/xiangmushow.html?id=883

http://www.longyou.gov.cn/art/2020/7/23/art_1242984_52188353.html

http://www.zjich.cn/xiangmu/xiangmushow.html?id=1095

https://www.qz123.com/html/297/20190504/news_show_218094.html

文化活动六：三月三祭祖典礼

Cultural Activity (6):

The Ancestor Worship Rituals on the Third Day of the Third Lunar Month

文化寻踪之浙里村落 Ancient Villages

➤ 建德市大慈岩镇新叶村
Xinye Village, Daciyan Town, Jiande City

新叶村位于浙江省建德市南部大慈岩镇，兰江与新安江之间。新叶村是中国目前保留完好的为数不多的古村落之一，也是中国最大的叶氏宗族聚居地。村落历史悠久，可追溯到南宋时期，距今已有800多年的历史。新叶村因其保留完好的生活习俗与住宅、祠堂、古塔等大量明清建筑，成为人们研究古村落布局、古建筑形制的教科书，素有“中国明清建筑露天博物馆”之美誉。

Xinye Village is located in Daciyan Town, south of Jiande City, Zhejiang Province, between the Lan River and the Xin’an River. It is one of the few ancient villages that have been well preserved, and the largest settlement of the Ye clan in China. The history of the village could be dated back to the Southern Song Dynasty, more than 800 years ago. Xinye Village has become a textbook for people to study the layout of ancient villages and the structure of ancient buildings because of its well-preserved living customs and houses, ancestral halls, ancient towers and many other Ming and Qing buildings. It is known as the "open-air museum of Chinese Ming and Qing architecture".

文化寻踪之浙里印记 Cultural Imprints

➢ 建筑文化
Architectural Culture

新叶祠堂 Xinye Ancestral Hall

新叶村的祠堂建筑数量多,记录了大量民俗信息。有序堂是玉华叶氏的总祠,位于村子的北端,是新叶村的结构中心,最早的住宅都建在它的两侧。西山祠堂是最早的祠堂,是玉华叶氏的祖庙,建于元代,如今已成为新叶小学的一部分。崇仁堂是新叶村最高大、最宽敞、最华丽的祠堂,它的规模不但超过了祖庙,而且超过了总祠。一般的祠堂只有两进或三进,而崇仁堂则有四进,总进深26米,纵深空间的神秘感非常强烈,这在中国的古建筑中很少见。

Xinye Village enjoys a large number of ancestral halls, with abundant historical folklore information recorded. Youxu Hall is the main ancestral hall of the Ye family, located at the northern end of the village. It is the structural center of the village as the earliest houses were built on the two sides of it. Xishan Ancestral Hall is the earliest one, and the ancestral temple of the Ye family. It was built in the Yuan Dynasty and has become a part of Xinye Primary School. Chongren Hall is the largest, most spacious, and most gorgeous ancestral hall. The general ancestral hall has only two or three rows of constructions, while Chongren Hall has four rows, with a total depth of 26 meters. The depth of the space creates a mysterious atmosphere, which is rare in the ancient Chinese architecture.

抟云塔建筑群 Tuanyun Pagoda Architectural Complex

新叶村的“塔”，叫作“抟云塔”，位于村口，始建于明隆庆年间（1567），落成于明万历二年（1575）。塔高38.8米，塔围13.8米，塔身像一支毛笔，传递着村民希望子孙后代文运亨通之意。村中的大街小巷以及农家的建筑陈设，基本上保持了百年前原有的风貌，齐整的砖条铺成的街巷，高耸的马头墙屋檐，以及老式木板门面上的精致木雕，都是明清朝代的产物。

Tuanyun Pagoda is located at the entrance of Xinye Village. It was first built in the reign of Emperor Longqing (1567) in the Ming Dynasty, and completed in the second year of Emperor Wanli (1575). The pagoda is 38.8 meters high and 13.8 meters in circumference. Since its shape is like a writing brush, the villagers believe it conveys a hope that the future generations will be excellent in learning and their career. The streets and alleys of the village and the architectural furnishings of the farmhouses mostly maintain the original style in a hundred years ago. The streets and lanes paved with neat bricks, the eaves of horse-head-shaped walls, and the exquisite wood carvings on the old wooden facades are all relics of the Ming and Qing Dynasties.

➢ 非遗文化
Intangible Cultural Heritage

新叶昆曲 Xinye Kunqu Opera

昆曲，除苏昆以外，还有在其他各地流布的地方支脉。新叶昆曲是清末金华昆曲流传并遗存在浙江省建德市新叶村的一脉。新叶昆曲算是昆剧园里的一朵“奇葩”，她带有些许泥土的气息，少了些宫廷脂粉气，有种别样的芬芳，有着“山香幽兰”的美称。

In addition to Suzhou Kunqu Opera, Kunqu Opera also has local branches spreading all over China. Among which, Xinye Kunqu Opera, originated from Jinhua Kunqu Opera at the end of the Qing Dynasty. Unlike the traditional Qunqu opera, Xinye Kunqu Opera is more close to the countryside life, therefore, it has been reputed as the “fragrant orchid in the moutain”.

新叶三月三 The Celebration on March 3rd (Lunar Calendar)

新叶三月三是浙西地区传统的迎神祭祖和集市等民俗活动的范本，具有活动规模大、参与人数多、乡土风味浓、内容丰富多彩等特点。每到三月三，新叶村都要举行大型的民俗活动，包括迎神、祭祖、赶集、社戏等，俗称“三月三”。

The celebration on March 3rd based on the lunar calendar is large-scale traditional folk activities, such as welcoming gods and worshiping ancestors in western Zhejiang. The celebration features enormous activities, a large number of participants, a strong local flavor and enriching contents. In Xinye Village, people will hold large-scale folklore activities, including welcoming the gods, worshiping ancestors, going to fairs, appreciating traditional operas, etc., commonly known as "March 3rd".

文化寻踪之出行贴士 Travel Tips

寻踪之旅载体：三月三祭祖典礼

寻踪之旅地点：浙江省建德市大慈岩镇新叶村

寻踪之旅时间：通常为4月

寻踪信息查询：(1)http://www.jdnews.com.cn；(2)"建德发布"微信公众平台；(3)搜狐、腾讯等多家网站。

Cultural Activity: The Ancestor Worship Rituals on the Third Day of the Third Lunar Month

Ancient Village: Xinye Village, Daciyan Town, Jiande City, Zhejiang Province

Travel Time: Usually in April

For More Information: (1) Please visit http://www.jdnews.com.cn; (2) Please search on the WeChat public platform "Jiande Fabu"; (3) Please visit the websites such as Sohu, Tencent, etc.

参考资料

http://hzjddxy.zjzwfw.gov.cn/art/2015/12/31/art_1010697_341877.html

http://www.huaxia.com/ly/fsmq/dl/2010/09/2075067.html
https://www.sohu.com/a/228189407_349225
http://gotrip.zjol.com.cn/05gotrip/system/2012/07/17/018663289.shtml
https://www.sohu.com/a/117725581_349157
http://www.xijucn.com/html/kunqu/20141114/62866.html
http://www.jdnews.com.cn/jdpd/whms/content/2009-07/15/content_2194909.html
https://yule.sohu.com/20140324/n397106241.shtml
http://www.zjjyzx.com/a/news/zhejiang/hangzhou/2015/0129/42932.html
http://jrjd.jdnews.com.cn/Article/index/aid/2804143.html
http://www.zjich.cn/xiangmu/xiangmushow.html?id=1450

May 5月

文化活动一：护国随粮王信俗会

Cultural Activity (1): The Patriotic King's Birthday Celebration

文化活动二：江山旅游

Cultural Activity (2): Best Time to Travel in Jiangshan

文化活动一：护国随粮王信俗会

Cultural Activity (1): The Patriotic King's Birthday Celebration

文化寻踪之浙里村落 Ancient Towns

➢ 嘉善县西塘镇
Xitang Town, Jiashan County

西塘镇，隶属浙江省嘉兴市嘉善县，位于江浙沪三地交界处。西塘历史悠久，是古代吴越文化的发祥地之一、江南六大古镇之一，被誉为"生活着的千年古镇"。西塘素以桥多、弄多、廊棚多而闻名，民风淳厚，橹声悠扬，到处可见中国古代传统文化特有的人文积淀。"春秋的水，唐宋的镇，明清的建筑，现代的人"，是对西塘最恰当不过的形容。

Xitang Town, under the jurisdiction of Jiashan County, Jiaxing City, Zhejiang Province, is situated in the joint part of Jiangsu, Zhejiang and Shanghai. Boasting a long history, Xitang is one of the birthplaces of ancient Wu-Yue culture and one of the six ancient towns in the south of the Yangtze River, reputed as "a thousand-year-old living town". Xitang is known for its abundant bridges, lanes, and ceilinged corridors. The people in the town are honest and warmhearted, while the sound of the sculls are melodious, all presenting a unique cultural accumulation of ancient Chinese traditional culture. "The water of spring and autumn, the town of the Tang and Song Dynasties, the architecture of the Ming and Qing Dynasties, and the people of modern society" perfectly depicts the ancient town—Xitang.

文化寻踪之浙里印记 Cultural Imprints

➤ 建筑文化
Architectural Culture

西塘古民居 Xitang Ancient Residential Buildings

明清时期，徽商东进，把徽派的文化和建筑技术带到西塘，西塘现存最好的民居就是这个时期建造的。民国时期，西塘已成为商业重镇。许多有钱人临河建屋，临街开店，留下了大规模的民居建筑。据2000年的普查，西塘镇尚有明、清和民国时期建造的民居建筑共25万余平方米，为中国江南水乡古镇之最。廊棚是西塘的一大特色，它是由沿街许多相邻的商店搭建连接而成的，全长1200多米。为了避免倭寇的犯扰，西塘古民居在沿街的门面是非常低调的，一般看不出大户人家的规模。在内部装饰上，西塘古民居表现得也颇为考究，门窗上每每刻有吉祥纹花，如"荷、梅"(谐音"和美")等，寄予美好含义。

During the Ming and Qing Dynasties, Huizhou merchants traveled eastward and introduced Huizhou culture and architectural techniques to Xitang. The best existing residences in Xitang were built during that period. In the years of the Republic of China, Xitang became a major commercial town. Many wealthy people built houses along the river and opened shops along the street, creating large-scale residential buildings. According to the census of 2000, there were more than 250,000 square meters of residential buildings built during the Ming and Qing Dynasties in Xitang, which is the largest among ancient water towns in the south of China. Xitang features abundant ceilinged corridors, which are connected by many adjacent shops along the street, spanning a total length of more than 1,200 meters. In order to avoid the harassment of Japanese pirates, the facades of Xitang ancient houses are very low-key, thus the scale of wealthy households is generally not visible. Xitang ancient residential buildings were decorated quite exquisitely interiorly, with the doors and windows often engraved with auspicious patterns, such as "lotus and plum blossoms" (the same with "harmonious and beautiful" in sound), which convey beautiful connotations.

非遗文化
Intangible Cultural Heritage

传统纽扣制作技艺 Traditional Button Making Skills

古色古香的纽扣博物馆就坐落在西塘镇老街小巷深处。在这里陈列着琳琅满目的古今纽扣和民国时期的制扣机器，小小的纽扣向人们述说着中国纽扣之乡美丽而久远的制扣历史。西塘镇的传统纽扣制作技艺主要有两种：

一种是贝壳纽扣，一种是布条编织的盘香纽扣。贝壳纽扣的原材料主要是产于当地的河蚌等。盘香纽扣一般用棉布、绸缎等布料制作而成，颜色花样根据服装色彩和主人喜爱而定。1996年，西塘镇被命名为“中国纽扣之乡”。

The quaint button museum is located deep in the old streets and alleys of Xitang Town. A dazzling array of ancient and modern buttons and button-making machines from the Republic of China are displayed here, telling people the beautiful and long history of button-making in the China's button town. There are two main traditional button making techniques in Xitang: one is shell button, and the other is Panxiang button woven from cloth strips. The raw materials of shell buttons are mainly local mussels, while Panxiang buttons are generally made of cotton, silk and other fabrics, with the color and patterns determined by the color of the clothes or the owner's preference. In 1996, Xitang Town was named the “hometown of buttons in China”.

八珍糕制作技艺 Bazhen Cake Making Skills

八珍糕是一种夏令防病食品，以糕内有八味中药成分而得名，产自嘉善县西塘镇。西塘钟介福药店是百年老店，所产八珍糕是创始人钟稻荪在1885年参考明代处方，结合临床经验，应用本地优质糯米和八味中药研制而成。八珍糕口感香甜松脆，蕴药理于食疗之中，食之无药味，既是药物，又是糕点佳品，成为嘉善特色药膳名点，深受当地百姓喜爱。

Bazhen cake is a summer disease-preventing food, which is named after the eight-flavor traditional Chinese medicine among the ingredients, and produced in Xitang Town, Jiashan County. Xitang Zhongjiefu Pharmacy is a century-old store, and its founder Zhong

Daosun first made the Bazhen cake in 1885 with reference to the prescription of the Ming Dynasty, and clinical experience, using local high-quality glutinous rice and eight Chinese medicines. Tasting sweet and crunchy, Bazhen cake applies pharmacology in the making process. It can be regarded as both medicine and delicacy, and therefore, has become a famous specialty medicated diet in Jiashan, prevailing among the locals.

京砖烧制技艺 Jing Brick Firing Technique

京砖烧制技艺是嘉善砖瓦烧制业中的独特传统工艺。嘉善砖瓦烧制业(俗称“窑业”)始于宋,兴于明,积数百年的烧制经验,形成了独特的烧制工艺。晚清至民国时期嘉善砖瓦烧制业规模很大,远近闻名。京砖烧制技艺被列入第三批浙江省非物质文化遗产名录。西塘镇对县内现存的唯一的和合窑进行了保护性修缮,修建了窑文化公园,建设了窑文化展示墙,以展现老一辈的制砖技艺。

Jiashan Jing brick firing technique is a unique traditional craft in the industry of Jiashan brick and tile firing (commonly known as “kiln industry”), which could date back to the Song Dynasty and flourished in the Ming Dynasty. With hundreds of years of firing experience, a unique firing technique had been formed in Jiashan. During the period from the late Qing Dynasty to the Republic of China, Jiashan’s brick and tile firing industry was well-known and large in scale. Jing brick firing technique was included in the third batch of Zhejiang Intangible Cultural Heritage List. Protective repairs has been carried out on the only existing Hehe kiln in the county, with the kiln culture park and display wall built as well to demonstrate the brick-making skills of the older generation.

嘉善宣卷 Jiashan Xuanjuan

宣卷是一种古老的民间说唱艺术，始于唐代，盛于明、清。在江浙沪一带漫长的流传发展过程中，它融入了各自地方的风俗、语言、唱腔、表演等，形成了各自不同的演唱特色。嘉善宣卷是浙江北部一种具有民间特色的曲艺样式，演出形式有木鱼宣卷和丝弦宣卷之分。木鱼宣卷盛行于19世纪中下叶，一般由二至三人演出。早年，去杭州、苏州、普陀山等地烧香的香客要坐手摇船去，路上需要多日，为了在旅途中增加欢乐，就请一班宣卷先生在香船里唱宣卷。后来发展到做寿等喜庆时日都请宣卷班去唱几场，以示庆贺。丝弦宣卷在20世纪30年代开始流行，是在木鱼宣卷的基础上发展而来的，有音乐器具配合。2012年6月，嘉善宣卷被列为浙江省第四批非物质文化遗产保护项目。

Xuanjuan is an ancient folk art of talking and singing that began in the Tang Dynasty and flourished in the Ming and Qing Dynasties. In the long process of spreading and developing in Jiangsu, Zhejiang and Shanghai, it integrated into the customs, language, singing, performance and other characteristics of their respective places, forming their own different singing characteristics. Jiashan Xuanjuan is a folk art style in northern Zhejiang, and the performances are divided into wooden fish Xuanjuan and silk string Xuanjuan. Wooden fish Xuanjuan was popular in the middle and late 19th century, usually performed by two to three people. In the early years, pilgrims who went to Hangzhou, Suzhou, Mount Putuo and other places to burn incense had to take a hand-cranked boat. In order to increase the joy of the long journey, a group of Xuanjuan performers were invited to sing on the boat. Gradually, the Xuanjuan troupes were frequently invited for celebration of birthday, etc. Silk string Xuanjuan became popular in the 1930s, which was developed on the basis of wooden fish Xuanjuan, accompanied by music instruments. In June 2012, Jiashan Xuanju was included in the fourth batch of intangible cultural heritage protection list in Zhejiang Province.

嘉善田歌 Jiashan Farming Song

田歌是农民间口耳相传的一种民歌，唱的是种田人的劳动、爱情和生活。被列入"国家级非物质文化遗产"的嘉善田歌传承于400多年前的明代吴歌(一种具有江南地方特色的民歌)。嘉善田歌共有7个曲调："平调""滴落声""急急歌""落秧歌""埭头歌""羊骚头""嗨啰调"。前3种曲调一般由一人演唱，后4种曲调由几个人有机配合，形成独唱、接唱、齐唱的特有形式。嘉善田歌的作者大多是不知名的百姓。它不仅具有鲜明的江南民歌特点，还富有嘉善地方特色。

Jiashan farming song is a kind of folk song passed down by the peasants, singing about labour, love and the farming life, etc., and was inherited from the Wu ballads (a folk song with local characteristics in the south of the Yangtze River) in the Ming Dynasty more than 400 years ago. It is included in the list of "National Intangible Cultural Heritage". The farming song consists of seven tunes: "level tune", "Di Luo Sheng", "Ji Ji song", "Luo Yang song", "Ditou song", "Yang Sao Tou" and "Hai Luo tune". The first three tunes are generally sung by one person, while the latter four tunes are organically coordinated by several people to form a unique performance of solo, sing, and unison. Jiashan farming song writers are mostly unknown civilians. It not only has the distinctive characteristics of folk songs, but also has the local features.

护国随粮王信俗会 The Patriotic King's Birthday Celebration

为祭奠明末放粮救民的随粮王，西塘百姓在他的生日四月初三举行盛大的赞神、娱神活动。此俗自清中后期至民国初形成，沿袭至今。庙会期间，四乡八邻的民众汇聚到西塘古镇，全镇商家营业通宵达旦，只为一场传承延续了一百多年的民间民俗活动——护国随粮王信俗会。信俗会分"出会"和"座会"两种，"出会"就是将随粮王神像抬出庙宇行街，出会一般分水路和陆路两组进行。四月初三已成为西塘人一年中最大的民间节日。

To pay homage to the Patriotic King, who distributed grain to save the people in the late Ming Dynasty, the people of Xitang hold grand praise and entertaining activities on the birthday of the Patriotic King each year, which is the third day of the fourth lunar month. This custom was formed from the middle and late Qing Dynasty to the beginning of the Republic of China and has been carried forward to the present. During the temple fair, people from nearby villages gathered in the ancient town of Xitang, and stores in the town were open all night long, only for a folk activity that has been passed down for more than a hundred years, the Patriotic King's birthday celebration. The activity is divided into two types, which are "Chuhui" (outside celebration) and "Zuohui" (inside celebration). "Chuhui" means to carry the statue of the king out of the temple and parade in waterway or roadway. Now the third day of the fourth lunar month has become the biggest folk festival for Xitang people throughout the year.

文化寻踪之出行贴士 Travel Tips

寻踪之旅载体:护国随粮王信俗会

寻踪之旅地点:浙江省嘉兴市嘉善县西塘镇

寻踪之旅时间:通常为5月

寻踪信息查询:(1)http://www.jsxww.cn/;(2)"西塘旅游"微信公众平台;(3)通过搜狐、腾讯等多家网站均可检索实时信息。

Cultural Activity: The Patriotic King's Birthday Celebration

Ancient Town: Xitang Town, Jiashan County, Jiaxing City, Zhejiang Province

Travel Time: Usually in May

For More Information: (1) Please visit http://www.jsxww.cn/; (2) Please search on the WeChat public platform "Xitang Lvyou"; (3) Please visit the websites such as Sohu, Tencent, etc.

参考资料

http://en.chinaculture.org/chineseway/2013-10/09/content_489342_3.htm

http://en.chinaculture.org/library/2003-09/24/content_36254.htm

http://jsb.jsxww.cn/html/jsb/20181120/jsb97617.html

http://jsb.jsxww.cn/Html/Jsb/20160311/Jsb72146.Html

http://gotrip. zjol. com. cn/xw14873/ycll14875/201805/t20180518_7297303.shtml

http://www.jiaxing.gov.cn/art/2014/1/13/art_1536221_22023203.html

http://jsb.jsxww.cn/Html/Jsb/20140808/Jsb57476.Html

http://jsxww.zjol.com.cn/jsnews/system/2010/12/06/012986652.shtml
http://jsxww.zjol.com.cn/jsnews/system/2010/11/09/012867926.shtml
http://jsxww.zjol.com.cn/jsnews/system/2010/11/01/012822330.shtml
http://jsxww.zjol.com.cn/jsnews/system/2009/12/30/011711500.shtml
http://jsxww.zjol.com.cn/jsnews/system/2010/10/19/012777704.shtml
http://www.jiashan.gov.cn/art/2017/8/24/art_1600397_28104318.html
http://travel.people.com.cn/n/2015/0707/c41570-27268071-8.html
https://www.sohu.com/a/205639106_664051
http://country.cnr.cn/xtxq/20140207/t20140207_514794031.shtml
http://feiyi.jxlib.com/content.asp?id=60&bid=7
http://feiyi.jxlib.com/content.asp?id=4&bid=1
http://en.chinaculture.org/2015-04/02/content_610181.htm
http://www.zjich.cn/xiangmu/xiangmushow.html?id=1132
http://www.zjich.cn/xiangmu/xiangmushow.html?id=862
http://www.zjich.cn/xiangmu/xiangmushow.html?id=1119
http://www.zjich.cn/xiangmu/xiangmushow.html?id=1473
http://www.zjich.cn/xiangmu/xiangmushow.html?id=297
http://www.zjich.cn/xiangmu/xiangmushow.html?id=1314
https://town.zjol.com.cn/czjsb/202102/t20210210_22106513.shtml

文化活动二：江山旅游

Cultural Activity (2): Best Time to Travel in Jiangshan

文化寻踪之浙里村落 Ancient Towns

➢ 江山市廿八都镇
Nianbadu Town, Jiangshan City

廿八都镇位于浙、闽、赣三省交界处，建镇已有900多年的历史。宋熙宁四年，江山设都四十四，此地排行二十八，故名。该地现存规模庞大且保存相对完整的明清古建筑群。主要有长约2公里的古街、36幢古民居和11幢古公共建筑，建筑风格融浙徽赣和客家式以及西洋式于一体。该镇有1.2万多人口，繁衍着142种姓氏，交流着13种方言，素有“百姓古镇”和“方言王国”之称。

Nianbadu is located at the junction of Zhejiang, Fujian and Jiangxi, spanning a history of more than 900 years. In the fourth year of Emperor Xining of the Song Dynasty, Jiangshan was sub-divided into forty-four towns. Ranking twenty-eighth, hence it had the name Nianbadu Town (the 28th town). The existing large-scale and relatively intact ancient buildings of the Ming and Qing Dynasties mainly include 2-kilometer-long ancient streets, 36 ancient residential buildings, 11 ancient public buildings, with the architectural style being a combination of Zhejiang, Anhui, Jiangxi, Hakka and Western styles. Boasting a population of more than 12,000, 142 family names, and 13 dialects, the town is known as the "ancient town of 100 surnames"and the "kingdom of dialects".

文化寻踪之浙里印记 Cultural Imprints

➢ 非遗文化
Intangible Cultural Heritage

廿八都木偶戏 Nianbadu Puppet Show

廿八都木偶戏经师徒相授，已经传承了18代约500年。该地木偶于明代自江西传入，故演唱唱腔均为赣剧属宜黄派。廿八都木偶造型十分精巧，它用坚韧的木料加工成型后，采用变形夸张的手法，进行彩绘、装潢，使之形神兼备，栩栩如生。现有剧目和现存木偶道具较多，对研究古代戏剧形式、表演艺术、唱腔、戏俗、民俗及戏剧发展史具有重大意义和较高的价值。

Nianbadu puppet show, taught in the way of master-apprentice, has been passed down for about 500 years throughout 18 generations. Introduced from Jiangxi in the Ming Dynasty, the lines and tunes take the form of the Yihuang school of Gan Opera.

Nianbadu puppets are very exquisite in shape. After being processed and shaped from tough wood, they are painted and decorated in a deformed and exaggerated way, creating the final lifelike puppets. There're many repertoires and various puppet props in existence in the town, which are of great significance and high value for the study of ancient drama forms, performing arts, singing, opera custom, folklore and the history of drama development.

廿八都山歌 Nianbadu Folk Song

明代以前因历代战争，均有军旅在廿八都屯扎。明清以来，商业发达，故这里成为商旅集散地，人口迅速集聚，有大量人口往廿八都迁移，因此廿八都成为一个移民部落。这些移民带来了各自的民歌、小调，在这个镇上进行文化交融。廿八都山歌就是在这样的社会文化背景下产生的。廿八都山歌表现形式多样、内容丰富，有反映生产、生活的，也有歌颂爱情、友情的，还有反映历史、社会的。廿八都山歌以对唱形式为主，歌词常带有即兴性。

Before the Ming Dynasty, due to wars in the past, there were military troops here. Since the Ming and Qing Dynasties, commerce has developed, so it has become a business and travel distribution center, and an immigrant town. These immigrants brought their own folk songs, ditties, and other cultural products which merged in the town, and fertilized the birth of Nianbadu folk songs. The folk songs are diversified in expressions and rich in content. The themes include production, life, love, friendship, history and society. The performing ways are mainly in the form of duet, while the lyrics are often impromptu.

文化寻踪之出行贴士 Travel Tips

寻踪之旅载体:江山旅游

寻踪之旅地点:浙江省江山市廿八都镇

寻踪之旅时间:通常为5月

寻踪信息查询:(1)http://www.js-news.cn/;(2)“江山发布”微信公众平台;(3)搜狐、腾讯等多家网站。

Cultural Activity: Best Time to Travel in Jiangshan

Ancient Town: Nianbadu Town, Jiangshan City, Zhejiang Province

Travel Time: Usually in May

For More Information: (1) Please visit http://www.js-news.cn/; (2) Please search on the WeChat public platform “Jiangshan Fabu”; (3) Please visit the websites such as Sohu, Tencent, etc.

参考资料

http://daj.qz.gov.cn/shtml/10266/460916/detail_1.shtml

https://www.sohu.com/a/331608197_184003

http://www.zjich.cn/xiangmu/xiangmushow.html?id=416

http://www.ihchina.cn/project_details/13450

https://www.sohu.com/a/199289877_99972930

http://www.zjich.cn/xiangmu/xiangmushow.html?id=619

https://zj.zjol.com.cn/news/406525.html?ismobilephone=1&t=1529386804634

https://www.sohu.com/a/112670365_383574

https://town. zjol. com. cn/gun/201904/t20190420_9946294. shtml? from=

timeline&isappinstalled=0

http://www.js-news.cn/xwzx/xzjd/202102/t20210201_3594818.html

June 6月

文化寻踪之推荐日历
Recommended Month

文化活动一：品慈城杨梅
Cultural Activity (1): Savouring the Waxberries

文化活动二：杨梅节
Cultural Activity (2): The Waxberries Festival

文化活动一：品慈城杨梅

Cultural Activity (1): Savouring the Waxberries

文化寻踪之浙里村落 Ancient Towns

➢ 江北区慈城镇

Cicheng Town, Jiangbei District

慈城位于宁波市江北区西北部，是江南地区唯一保存得较为完整的古县城，保存了完整的传统生活结构方式。唐开元二十六年（738）始设慈溪县以来，慈城一直为县治所在。宋时慈城始筑城墙，现城区格局形成于明代。全城的道路网由“三纵”“四横”组成，形成规整的棋盘形平面格局，这种格局在我国江南现存古城中仅此一例，是慈城的一大特点。慈城保存了大批明清祠庙、官宅民居、牌坊等古建筑，具有较高的历史研究价值。

Located in the northwest of Jiangbei District, Ningbo City, Cicheng Town is the only well-preserved ancient county in the south of the

Yangtze River, which keeps a complete traditional life style. Since the establishment in the 26th year of Emperor Kaiyuan's reign (738), the Tang Dynasty, Cicheng has always been the political center of the county. In the Song Dynasty, Cicheng began to build a city wall, while the current urban structure was formed in the Ming Dynasty. The road network of the whole town is composed of three vertical and four horizontal road ways, forming a regular checkerboard-shaped plane pattern, which is the only example among the existing ancient cities in the south region of the Yangtze River, and therefore, becomes a major feature of Cicheng. The town boasts a large number of ancient buildings with a high value of historical research, such as Ming and Qing ancestral temples, official residences and local dwellings, memorial archways, etc.

文化寻踪之浙里印记 Cultural Imprints

➢ 建筑文化
Architectural Culture

慈城古建筑群 Cicheng Ancient Building Complex

慈城保留下来的传统建筑中不但有大量的民居建筑，而且有孔庙、会馆、牌坊、古井等公共建筑、构筑物。其中孔庙布局完整，规模宏大，为浙东地区现存最为完整的文庙，反映了儒学在传统生活中的重要性及其深远的影响。这里的名人故居，做工精致，用料考究，是当地民居的代表作。其周围仍保留了完整的传统街区，集中反映了慈城明清时期建筑风格和生活气息。冯岳彩绘台门是江南彩绘的重要实例,具有宋式彩画的遗风。2006年6月,慈城古建筑群被国务院公布为第六批全国重点文物保护单位。2009年,其获联合国"文化遗产保护荣誉奖"。

Among the traditional buildings preserved in Cicheng, there are not only a large number of residential buildings but also public buildings and structures such as Confucian Temple, guildhalls, archways, and ancient wells, etc., of which Confucian Temple is complete in layout and large in scale. It is the most complete Confucian temple in eastern Zhejiang, reflecting the importance and far-reaching influence of Confucianism in the traditional life. Boasting exquisite workmanship, sophisticated materials, the former residences of celebrities are representative works of local dwellings, and the surrounding traditional blocks are still well preserved, reflecting the architectural style and life atmosphere of Cicheng during the Ming and Qing Dynasties. Feng Yue's painted Taimen residence, the traditional dwelling, is an important example in the south of the Yangtze River, with the legacy of Song-style colored drawings. In June 2006, Cicheng ancient building complex was announced by the State Council as the sixth batch of national key cultural relics protection units. In 2009, it won the "Cultural Heritage Protection Honor Award" from the United Nations.

非遗文化
Intangible Cultural Heritage

水磨年糕手工制作技艺 Handmade Skills of Water Mill Rice Cakes

年糕,作为谢年祭祀的供品,含"年年高"的意思,被列为宁绍地区的食点之首。相传是大禹治水给浙江百姓带来实惠,大家就将在整好的水田上种出来的粮食做成糕祭祀他。宁波制作年糕历史悠久，在北宋已有用米粉做糕的记述。水磨年糕的味道好，但工序复杂。

Nian'gao (rice cake), as an offering for the New Year sacrifice, embodies the meaning of "becoming better year by year", and is listed as the top food choice in Ningbo and Shaoxing areas. Legend has it that after Da Yu, a legendary Chinese hero, tamed the rivers and made them beneficial to farming in the prehistorical era, people in Zhejiang used the food produced on the paddy fields to make rice cake for sacrifice. Ningbo enjoys a long history of making rice cake, and rice flours had been used to make cake in the Northern Song Dynasty. The taste of water mill rice cake is delicous; however, the process is relatively complicated.

骨木镶嵌技艺 Bone Wood Inlay Technique

大约隋唐时，宁波出现了骨木镶嵌工艺品。宁波骨木镶嵌是民间工艺与家具、建筑相结合的一种装饰形式，包括传统家具、生活用品、门窗建筑装饰等，以牛骨片、木片等为原料用钢丝锯锯出各种纹饰，在木坯上起槽后用黄鱼胶粘结嵌入花纹，再经打磨雕刻、髹漆而成。在制作方法上有高嵌、平嵌、高平混嵌三种。常用的题材以历史故事、民间传说、生活风俗、和合二仙、梅兰竹菊等带有吉祥寓意的图案为主，与中华民族传统文化一脉相承，内容丰富多彩。

Bone wood inlay technique first emerged in Ningbo around the time of the Sui and Tang Dynasties. The technique is a decorative form that combines folk crafts with furniture and architecture, including traditional furniture, daily necessities, door and window architectural decorations, etc. It uses beef bone chips and wood chips as raw materials to be sawed into various patterns with a steel wire. After grooves are formed on the wooden billet, the yellow croaker gelatin is used to bond and embed the patterns, followed by the process of polishing, carving and painting. Commonly used themes are mostly historical stories, folklore, life customs, bamboo, chrysanthemum and other patterns with auspicious connotations, which are in the same line with the traditional Chinese culture and have rich and colorful contents.

文化寻踪之出行贴士 Travel Tips

寻踪之旅载体:品慈城杨梅

寻踪之旅地点:浙江省宁波市江北区慈城镇

寻踪之旅时间:通常为6月

寻踪信息查询:(1)http://www.nbjb.gov.cn/;(2)“行走慈城”微信公众平台;(3)搜狐、腾讯等多家网站。

Cultural Activity: Savouring the Waxberries

Ancient Town: Cicheng Town, Jiangbei District, Ningbo City, Zhejiang Province

Travel Time: Usually in June

For More Information: (1) Please visit http://www.nbjb.gov.cn/; (2) Please search on the WeChat public platform “Xingzou Cicheng”; (3) Please visit the websites such as Sohu, Tencent, etc.

参考资料

https://www.sohu.com/a/224978867_467457
https://www.sohu.com/a/193057806_814969

http://www.zjich.cn/xiangmu/xiangmulist.html?keyword=%u9AA8%u6728%u9576%u5D4C
http://www.zjich.cn/xiangmu/xiangmushow.html?id=1093
http://www. ce. cn/culture/whcyk/gundong/201107/18/t20110718_22548099.shtml
http://theory.people.com.cn/n/2013/1216/c107503-23845305.html
https://www.163.com/dy/article/G9L3E0PV053997FP.html
https://new.qq.com/rain/a/20210509A001JL00
http://www.zjich.cn/news/newsshow.html?id=433784

文化活动二：杨梅节

Cultural Activity (2): The Waxberries Festival

文化寻踪之浙里村落 Ancient Towns

➢ 松阳县西屏镇

Xiping Town, Songyang County

西屏镇是松阳县人民政府所在地，是松阳县的政治、经济、文化中心。西屏山奇水秀，不仅自然条件优越，还是一个有着1100多年历史的古镇。瓯江支流松荫溪穿城而过，城西2公里处，有始建于北宋、现为国家级重点保护文物的延庆寺塔。西屏是宋代四大女词人之一张玉娘的出生地，现存历史遗迹鹦鹉冢。

Xiping Town is the seat of Songyang County People's Government and the political, economic and cultural center of the county. Xiping Town boasts magnificent mountains and beautiful rivers, with superior natural conditions, and a history of more than 1,100 years. The Songyin Stream, a branch of the Ou River, runs through the town; two kilometers to the west of the town is Yanqing Temple Pagoda, which was built in the Northern Song Dynasty and is now a national key cultural relic; Xiping is the birthplace of Zhang Yuniang, one of the four great female poets of the Song Dynasty, with the historical sites, Parrot Tomb, in memory of the legendary stories.

文化寻踪之浙里印记 Cultural Imprints

➢ 建筑文化
Architectural Culture

延庆寺塔 Yanqing Temple Pagoda

延庆寺塔于北宋咸平二年(999)动工兴建,于咸平五年建成。因塔址在云龙山下延庆寺前,故以寺取名。1000多年来,延庆寺塔没有发现后人修缮的痕迹,是江南诸塔中保留最完整的北宋遗物,被誉为“江南稀宝”“浙江第一塔”。该塔塔身微斜仍屹立不倒,故又被称作“东方的比萨斜塔”。2006年,延庆寺塔被国务院公布为全国重点文物保护单位。

Yanqing Temple Pagoda was built in the second year of Xianping in the Northern Song Dynasty (999) and completed in the fifth year of Xianping. The pagoda is located in front of Yanqing Temple, at the foot of Mountain Yunlong, therefore, it is named after Yanqing Temple. For more than a thousand years, no repair traces have been found on Yanqing Temple pagoda by the later generations, and it is the most intact relic of the

Northern Song Dynasty among the pagodas in the south of the Yangtze River. It is reputed as "the rare treasure in the south of the Yangtze River" and "the best pagoda in Zhejiang". Being slightly leaning, the pagoda is also known as the "Leaning Tower of Pisa in the East". In 2006, it was announced as a national key cultural relics protection unit by the State Council.

非遗文化
Intangible Cultural Heritage

松阳高腔 Songyang High-Pitched Singing

松阳高腔是浙江省稀有剧种之一，源于宋元南戏，被誉为戏曲的活化石。于元末明初成演，清乾隆、道光年间颇为兴盛。松阳高腔原有唱腔曲牌108首，剧目丰富。2006年，松阳高腔被列入首批国家级非物质文化遗产保护名录。

Songyang high-pitched singing is one of the rare operas in Zhejiang Province. Originated from the Southern Opera of the Song and Yuan Dynasties, a kind of local classical opera in South China, it is reputed as the living fossil of opera. Songyang high-pitched singing was performed in the late Yuan Dynasty and the early Ming Dynasty, and flourished during the Qianlong and Daoguang years of the Qing Dynasty. Songyang high-pitched singing has 108 original tunes with a rich repertoire. In 2006, it was listed in the first batch of national intangible cultural heritage protection lists.

松阳端午茶 Songyang Dragon Boat Festival Tea

松阳端午茶，是以藿香、野菊、桑叶、菖蒲、山苍柴、鱼腥草等配制而成的养生饮品，因每逢端午佳节，百姓上山采选百草，晾制家中常年备饮而得名。在长期预防疾病与保健的过程中，松阳先民根据本地的气候、水土的特性，以草药为基础，融入中医养生，创造了具有独特配方的民间草药茶饮。

Songyang Dragon Boat Festival tea is a wholesome herbal drink made from agastache, wild chrysanthemum, mulberry leaves, calamus, houttuynia cordata, etc. During the Dragon Boat Festival, the locals go to mountains to pick herbs and dry them for the drinking throughout the year. In the process of long-term disease prevention and health care, Songyang's ancestors created the folk herbal tea with a unique formula based on the local climate, water, soil characteristics, and traditional Chinese medicine.

文化寻踪之出行贴士 Travel Tips

寻踪之旅载体：杨梅节

寻踪之旅地点：浙江省丽水市松阳县西屏镇

寻踪之旅时间：通常为6月

寻踪信息查询：(1)http://www.songyang.gov.cn/；(2)"松阳文旅"微信公众平台；(3)搜狐、腾讯等多家网站。

Cultural Activity: The Waxberries Festival

Ancient Town: Xiping Town, Songyang County, Lishui City, Zhejiang Province

Travel Time: Usually in June

For More Information: (1) Please visit http://www. songyang. gov. cn/; (2) Please search on the WeChat public platform "Songyang Wenlv"; (3) Please visit the websites such as Sohu, Tencent, etc.

参考资料

http://gotrip.zjol.com.cn/201801/t20180104_6249417.shtml

http://www.songyang.gov.cn/

http://xt.inlishui.com/html/2010/lsgj_0906/244.html

https://www. songyangwlt. com/company/scenic/391d3745-5dff-4992-bcda-8145411a2676/about

http://syxww.zjol.com.cn/syxww/system/2010/06/30/012314129.shtml

http://www.zjda.gov.cn/art/2014/1/16/art_1388591_12533299.html

http://www.ihchina.cn/project_details/13150/

https://m.sohu.com/a/240184706_100015102/

http://syxww.zjol.com.cn/syxww/system/2017/06/22/030192118.shtml

https://www.sohu.com/a/400311228_120054497

https://www.sohu.com/a/236178595_99918861

文化活动一：岱山东沙镇弄堂节

Cultural Activity (1): Alley Festival in Dongsha Town, Daishan

文化活动二：古村文化旅游节（永兴庙会）

Cultural Activity (2): Ancient Village Cultural Tourism Festival (Yongxing Temple Fair)

7月 July

文化活动一：岱山东沙镇弄堂节

Cultural Activity (1):

Alley Festival in Dongsha Town, Daishan

文化寻踪之浙里村落 Ancient Towns

➢ 岱山县东沙镇

Dongsha Town, Daishan County

东沙镇建制于唐，兴盛于清。清康熙年间，每逢鱼汛各地渔船聚集东沙，船以千计，人达数万。遂以渔兴市，以市兴镇，东沙成为中国东部沿海著名的渔业商埠。悠久的历史，繁荣的商贸，形成了东沙镇特有的文化底蕴与人文内涵。

Dongsha Town was established in the Tang Dynasty and prospered in the Qing Dynasty. During the reign of Emperor Kangxi of the Qing Dynasty, thousands of fishing boats and tens of thousands of people gathered in Dongsha during the fishing season. The fishing industry boosted the development of the market, while the market boosted the town, and gradually Dongsha became a famous fishery commercial port along the eastern coast of China. The long history and prosperous commerce have formed Dongsha Town's unique culture and humanistic connotations.

文化寻踪之浙里印记 Cultural Imprints

➤ 非遗文化 Intangible Cultural Heritage

舟山渔民号子 Zhoushan Fishermen's Songs

舟山渔民号子，是舟山群岛各类渔船工号子的总称，是世代以海为生的舟山渔民和船工在大海和岸上劳作中创作形成、不断丰富并世代相传的民间口头音乐。起于唐宋，兴于清，在二十世纪六七十年代仍呈鼎盛之势，其产生和发展与传统渔业息息相关，曲调粗犷优美，品种相对齐全，在全省乃至国内沿海地区的民间劳动号子中具有鲜明的代表性。

Zhoushan fishermen's song, the general name of various fishermen and boatmen's chants in the Zhoushan Archipelago, is a marine folk oral music created by Zhoushan fishermen and boatmen who have spent generations working on the sea, and has been enriched and passed on throughout the history. Originated in the Tang and Song Dynasties and flourished in the Qing Dynasty, it was still at its peak in 1960s and 1970s. The tunes of Zhoushan fishermen and boatmen's song are rough and beautiful, and its variety is relatively complete, which has made its fame in the work songs of the whole country.

舟山锣鼓 Zhoushan Gong and Drum

舟山丰富的海洋资源和特定的生产方式、生活习俗孕育了独特的民间艺术,舟山锣鼓就是其中的代表。旧时的舟山锣鼓大多出现在村里的红白喜事、庙会庆典及渔民祭海等活动中。在1957年莫斯科举办的世界青年联欢节上,舟山锣鼓曾荣获世界民间音乐比赛金质奖章。舟山锣鼓乐器配制齐全,其中的两大主奏乐器,分别是由十三面锣组成的排锣和由五面鼓组成的排鼓,其演奏风格独特,音量对比鲜明,音色丰富。

Zhoushan's rich marine resources, special modes of production and living custom have nurtured unique folk arts, and among which Zhoushan gongs and drums are the representatives. In the old days, they were mostly used in ceremonial occasions, temple fairs, and fishermen's offerings to the sea in villages. At the World Festival of Youth and Students held in Moscow in 1957, Zhoushan gongs and drums won the gold medal of the World Folk Music Competition. Zhoushan gongs and drums have a complete set of instruments. The two main instruments are the row of gongs composed of thirteen gongs and the row of drums composed of five drums. The playing style is unique, the volume contrast is sharp, and the timbre is rich.

岱山布袋木偶戏 Daishan Pop-Pocket Puppet Show

岱山布袋木偶戏,当地又称"小戏文",是一种起源于17世纪中国福建泉州或漳洲的一种用布偶来表演的地方戏剧,于150多年前由宁波人朱潭山传入舟山。表演分前后场,前场艺人操数个木偶在戏台上表演,后场艺人组成乐团进行伴奏,共同完成一段剧目的表演。布袋木偶戏具有

技巧高超、造型精美的特点，尤为擅长武打场面和刻画人物性格。岱山布袋木偶戏唱腔以“二簧”为主，配合其他戏曲声腔，后来吸收岱山方言、民间流行小调等，形成一种岱山独特的民间戏剧表演形式，表演内容以历史剧为主。

Daishan pop-pocket puppet show, also known locally as “micro drama”, is a kind of local drama performed with puppets originated in Quanzhou or Zhangzhou, Fujian, China in the 17th century. It was introduced to Zhoushan by Zhu Tanshan from Ningbo over 150 years ago. The performance is divided into the front and back stages. The artists at the front stage perform several puppets on the stage, and the artists at the back stage play accompaniment on musical instruments, working with each other to complete a performance together. The show has the characteristics of superb skills and exquisite modeling, and is especially good at the scenes of playing Kungfu fighting and portraying characters, therefore, the performance is mainly about historical drama. The operatic tunes of Daishan pop-pocket puppet show were dominated by “Erhuang” tune, combined with other operatic tunes, and later absorbed Daishan dialect and popular minor tunes, forming a unique form of folk drama performance in Daishan.

祭海 Sea Worship Ceremony

祭海是舟山渔民崇拜和信仰海龙王及海上诸神的一种祭祀方式，是中国东海海洋文化史上最具海洋文化个性的民俗之一。旧时由于生产工具落后，渔民在海上的人身安全受到了极大威胁，于是他们将传说中的海上诸神明奉为生命保护神和丰收的赐福神，形成了“出海祭龙王、丰收谢龙王、求雨靠龙王”的龙崇拜、龙信仰氛围。祭海有开捕祭、谢洋祭、庆丰祭、新船祭等。每逢鱼汛开洋、谢洋时节均要举行祭海仪式。传承下来的祭海习俗,如今仍保留着粗犷、纯朴的原生态文化风貌,展现着东海渔民龙信仰的独特传统民俗与深厚文化内涵。

Offering sacrifice to the sea is a way for Zhoushan fishermen to show their worship and believe in the sea dragon king and sea gods, which is also one of the most unique folk customs of marine culture throughout the history in the East China Sea area. In the old days, the personal safety of fishermen on the sea was greatly threatened due to the backward production tools. Therefore, the legendary sea gods were regarded as the gods of life protection and the blessing of harvest, and the atmosphere of the dragon worship and the dragon belief was gradually formed, i.e. "offering sacrifice to the sea dragon for a safe fishing journey, a big harvest and sufficient rainfall". Sea worship ceremony is held during fishing seasons on both the beginning day and the ending day. Through inheritance, the custom of offering sacrifice to the sea still retains the crude and simple original ecological cultural features, showing the unique traditional folk custom and profound cultural connotations of the dragon belief among the fishermen of the East China Sea.

文化寻踪之出行贴士 Travel Tips

寻踪之旅载体:岱山东沙镇弄堂节
寻踪之旅地点:浙江省舟山市岱山县东沙镇
寻踪之旅时间:通常为7月中下旬

寻踪信息查询：(1)http://www.daishan.gov.cn；(2)"东沙旅游"微信公众平台；(3)搜狐、腾讯等多家网站。

Cultural Activity: Alley Festival in Dongsha Town, Daishan

Ancient Town: Dongsha Town, Daishan County, Zhoushan City, Zhejiang Province

Travel Time: Usually mid to late July

For More Information: (1) Please visit http://www.daishan.gov.cn; (2) Please search on the WeChat public platform "Dongsha Lvyou"; (3) Please visit the websites such as Sohu, Tencent, etc.

参考资料

http://news.sohu.com/20160902/n467440031.shtml

http://www.zjfeiyi.cn/xiangmu/xiangmushow.html?id=313

http://www.zjfeiyi.cn/xiangmu/xiangmushow.html?id=205

http://www.zjfeiyi.cn/xiangmu/xiangmushow.html?id=888

http://www.zjfeiyi.cn/xiangmu/xiangmushow.html?id=831

https://baijiahao.baidu.com/s?id=1640164573941124634&wfr=spider&for=pc

http://xxgk.zhoushan.gov.cn/art/2018/7/16/art_1277198_19534298.html

https://baike.baidu.com/item/%E4%B8%9C%E6%B2%99%E9%95%87/1808638?fr=aladdin

http://zjnews.zjol.com.cn/05zjnews/system/2012/12/25/019041841.shtml

http://www.zjfeiyi.cn/zaiti/zaitishow.html?id=751

http://www.daishan.gov.cn/art/2017/8/22/art_1326439_9739472.html

http://www.ihchina.cn/project_details/12534

http://www.daishan.gov.cn/art/2018/7/17/art_1453736_19509832.html

http://zjzs.wenming.cn/zswh/201606/t20160616_2629098.htm

https://zj.zjol.com.cn/news/985761.html

https://new.qq.com/omn/20190728/20190728A0IA9Y00.html?pc
http://jrdh.zjol.com.cn/html/2017-04/14/content_174778.htm

文化活动二：古村文化旅游节（永兴庙会）

Cultural Activity (2):

Ancient Village Cultural Tourism Festival (Yongxing Temple Fair)

文化寻踪之浙里村落 Ancient Villages

➢ 绍兴市稽东镇冢斜村
Zhongxie Village, Jidong Town, Shaoxing City

冢斜村地处绍兴南部山区的稽东镇，离市区30多公里，北靠大龙山，南临舜江，是绍兴市首个获得"中国历史化名村"称号的古村落。"冢"是墓，"斜"是宫人墓，相传越国宫人多葬于此，墓不正向，故名曰"斜"，冢斜村名因此而来。冢斜村至今仍保存着丰富的历史文化遗迹，以及富有地方特色的民居、祠堂、古井等，是江南古村落的典型代表。

Zhongxie Village is located in Jidong Town, a mountainous area in southern Shaoxing. It is more than 30 kilometers away from the urban area, with the Dalong Mountain in the north and the Shun River in the south. It is the first ancient village in Shaoxing City to be awarded the title of "Chinese Historical Famous Village". The character "Zhong" means the tomb, and "Xie" refers to the tomb of the palace servants. Legend has it that, most of the palace servants of the Yue Kingdom were buried here, and the tomb was not facing upright, hence, the tomb is named "Xie", which also was the origin of the village's name. Until today, Zhongxie Village still preserves many historical and cultural sites, and civilian residences, ancestral halls and ancient wells with local characteristics, making it a typical representative of ancient villages in the south of the Yangtze River.

文化寻踪之浙里印记 Cultural Imprints

➤ 建筑文化 Architectural Culture

永兴公祠 Yongxing Ancestral Hall

永兴公祠位于绍兴市稽东镇冢斜村，当地村民更喜欢把它叫作永兴庙。其始建于唐朝贞元九年(793)，是为纪念被唐太宗称为"身兼五绝"的大书法家、大诗人虞世南而建的。永兴公祠坐落在冢斜村大龙山南麓，坐北朝南，建筑面积为1045平方米。公祠结构为二进，正殿中间为虞世南(众称永兴大王)塑像，高3米，笑容可掬，塑像上方悬挂虞世南的手迹"攀龙附凤"(仿制)横匾。前殿还悬挂明代礼部尚书汤金钊的"和风降福"和清代名臣余炳焘的"玉帛朝宗"等横匾。后殿有如来大佛，大佛两旁有火神、观世童等佛像，大佛后面有山神菩萨。

寻找浙里的乡愁印记——浙江古村落文化寻踪

浙江

Yongxing Ancestral Hall, or preferably, known as Yongxing Temple by the locals, is located in Zhongxie Village, Jidong Town, Shaoxing City. First built in the 9th year of Zhenyuan (793) in the Tang Dynasty, the ancestral hall was to commemorate the great calligrapher and poet Yu Shinan, who was called as the possessor of "Five Unique Skills" by the Emperor Taizong of the Tang Dynasty. Yongxing Ancestral Hall is situated at the southern foot of the Dalong Mountain in the village and facing south, with a construction area of 1, 045 square meters. Yongxing Ancestral Hall consists of two halls in total. In the middle of the front hall is the statue of Yu Shinan (commonly known as King Yongxing), which is 3 meters high. And you can see a pleasant smile on his face. Above the statue is a horizontal plaque with Yu Shinan's handwriting "Pan Long Fu Feng" (replica), meaning "to serve an Emperor and do service for a throne". The front hall also hangs horizontal inscribed boards such as "He Feng Jiang Fu" (meaning "a gentle wind brings fortune") written by Tang Jinzhao, the Ministry of Rituals of the Ming Dynasty, and "Yu Bo Chao Zong" (meaning "jade objects and silk fabrics for the emperor") written by Yu Bingtao, a famous official of the Qing Dynasty. There is a Tathagata Buddha statue in the back hall, and behind is the Mountain God Bodhisattva.

余氏宗祠 Yu's Ancestral Hall

余氏宗祠又称明德堂，始建于清朝乾隆年间，坐北朝南，四合院式，总面积约560平方米，保存完整。宗祠的两边大门上画着门神。宗祠门前立有两块分别刻有"文魁"和"恩科"的旗杆石板。祠堂内分为两进，在祠堂里面有一座颇为精致的戏台。这座古戏台建筑考究，雕饰华丽。中国著名越剧表演艺术大师袁雪芬曾经在这里登台演出。余氏宗祠是余氏后代祭奠祖宗的场所，记录了两百多年来余氏一族的兴衰，是研究江南宗祠建筑的重要依据。

Yu's Ancestral Hall, also known as Mingde Hall, was built during the reign of Emperor Qianlong in the Qing Dynasty. The wall faces south and sits in a courtyard style with a total area of about 560 square meters and is well preserved so far. Door gods are painted on both sides of the gates of the ancestral hall, which are the most popular patron saints and are believed to drive away evil spirits for villagers. Two flagpole slates with "Wen Kui" and "En Ke" inscribed in front of the ancestral hall. The ancestral hall is composed of two halls. Inside there is a rather delicate ancient stage, with sophisticated architecture and gorgeous carvings. The famous Yueju Opera performer Yuan Xuefen once performed here. Yu's Ancestral Hall is a place, where the descendants of the Yu family pay homage to their ancestors. This place records the rise and fall of the Yu family for more than two hundred years. It serves as an important basis for studying the architecture of the ancestral halls in the south of the Yangtze River.

余氏老台门 Yu's Ancient Taimen

余氏老台门始建于明崇祯十六年(1643)，占地面积886平方米。台门坐北朝南，共有三进，两侧厢，楼上相互贯通，均为二层楼。第一进和第二进设有穿堂，可以直至第三进最后一堂，至今保护完整。据说清朝名臣余炳焘就出生于老台门。余氏老台门是冢斜最早的以台门格局造就的居民房屋群。台门古朴，生活和生产痕迹明显。

Yu's Ancient Taimen, a type of traditional dwellings in Shaoxing, was built in the 16th year of Emperor Chongzhen (1643) in the Ming Dynasty, covering an area of 886 square meters. Sitting in the north and facing south, the Taimen has three rows of buildings with wing rooms on both sides, all of which are two-story buildings and the upper floors are connected to each other. The hallways are provided to reach the last row of buildings. It is said that Yu Bingtao, a famous official of the Qing Dynasty, was born in the ancient Tiamen. Yu's Ancient Taimen is the earliest residential housing complex in the form of Taimen structure in Zhongxie. The Taimen is full of simplicity, with dense traces of life and production.

高新屋台门 Gaoxinwu Taimen

高新屋台门位于冢斜村中部，始建于清乾隆五十年(1785)，占地面积985平方米。该台门坐北朝南，前后两进，内设大院，置东西侧厢。院内采用山区特有的鹅卵石铺面，楼上第一进建有旱街。该屋地域特色明显，构建讲究，保存完整。

Located in the middle of Zhongxie Village, Gaoxinwu Taimen was first built in the 50th year of Emperor Qianlong (1785) of the Qing Dynasty, covering an area of 985 square meters. The Taimen sits on the north and faces the south, and has two rows of constructions and a big courtyard inside, with wing rooms on both east and west sides. The courtyard is paved with cobblestones that are unique to mountainous areas, and there are dry street upstairs in the first row of buildings. Generally, Gaoxinwu Taimen has obvious regional characteristics, exquisite construction and complete preservation.

➢ 名人文化
Celebrity Culture

状元余煌 Yu Huang, No.1 Scholar in the Highest Imperial Examination)

余煌(1588—1646),字武贞,号公逊,浙江会稽人。明天启五年(1625)状元,曾任翰林院修撰,南明鲁王政权的兵部尚书,绍兴著名乡贤。余煌自幼有大志,好学,博览群书。他为人操行坚正,耿直不阿,一生爱国爱民爱家乡。隆武二年(1646)六月,清兵直逼绍兴,鲁王渡海而逃。余煌见大势已去,果断下令,大开城门,放军民出城避难。城空之后他赋绝命诗一首,独自出东门赴水,殉国而死。

Yu Huang (1588-1646), courtesy name Wuzhen and art name Gongxun, was born in Kuaiji, Zhejiang. He was No. 1 scholar in the highest imperial examination in the fifth year of Tianqi (1625) of the Ming Dynasty, and once worked as the minister of the Ministry of War for the King of Lu in the Southern Ming Dynasty, and was the famous village scholar of Shaoxing. Yu Huang had great ambition since childhood. He was eager to learn and read widely. Being an upright and honest person, he loved the country, the people, and his hometown throughout his life. In June of the second year of Longwu (1646), the soldiers of the Qing Dynasty pressed up to Shaoxing, and the King of Lu crossed the sea and fled. The situation was so hopeless that Yu Huang decisively gave the order to open the city gates and let the soldiers and civilians go out of city to take refuge. After the city was evacuated, he wrote his last poem, went out from the east gate alone, and threw into river for his country.

河南布政使余炳焘 Yu Bingtao, Exchequer of Henan

余炳焘(? —1857),字吟香,浙江会稽人,冢斜余氏后裔,清朝名臣。道光元年举人,充景山官学教习期满,以知县用,分发陕西,官至河南布政使。他身患重病,仍继续在战场指挥作战,不久病逝,其事迹载入国史。

Yu Bingtao (?–1857), courtesy name Yinxiang, was born in Kuaiji, Zhejiang. He was a descendant of the Yu clan of Zhongxie and a famous official of the Qing Dynasty. He was a provincial graduate of the first year of Emperor Daoguang (1821), and served as the teacher of Jingshan Official Study. After his employment period ends, he was hired as the county magistrate and assigned to Shaanxi. His highest position as an official was exchequer of Henan. Although he was seriously ill, he continued to command operations on the battlefield, which led to his later death due to overwork. His deeds had gone down in the history of the country.

文化寻踪之出行贴士 Travel Tips

寻踪之旅载体:古村文化旅游节(永兴庙会)

寻踪之旅地点:浙江省绍兴市稽东镇冢斜村

寻踪之旅时间:通常为7月

寻踪信息查询:(1)http://www.sx.gov.cn/;(2)"冢斜古村"微信公众平台;(3)搜狐、腾讯等多家网站。

Cultural Activity: Ancient Village Cultural Tourism Festival (Yongxing Temple Fair)

Ancient Village: Zhongxie Village, Jidong Town, Shaoxing City, Zhejiang Province

Travel Time: Usually in July

For More Information: (1) Please visit http://www.sx.gov.cn/; (2) Please search on the WeChat public platform "Zhongxie Gucun"; (3) Please visit the websites such as Sohu, Tencent, etc.

参考资料

https://zjnews.zjol.com.cn/05zjnews/system/2006/04/07/006557835.shtml

http://www.360doc.com/content/15/0414/20/11005683_463209655.shtml

https://www.bilibili.com/video/av63690803/

http://www.hang-zhou.net/sxzixun/20170306/5905.html

https://www.sohu.com/a/128184475_525464

http://www.chinaknowledge.de/History/Terms/buzhengshi.html

http://www.chinaknowledge.de/History/Rep/rep-government.html#usurpers

https://www.meipian.cn/3wc84tf

https://cs.zjol.com.cn/tszc/201906/t20190602_10250314.shtml

http://www.jiapuweb.com/html/20161122/n99627133.html

https://www.meipian.cn/428g0ar

http://yu1.zupu.cn/wenhua/349111.jhtml

http://www.hang-zhou.net/sxzixun/20170306/5905.html

http://www.hang-zhou.net/sxzixun/20170306/5905.html

http://www.360doc.com/content/19/0304/09/6657566_819065266.shtml

https://dy.163.com/article/FMVEQ230051296DE.html

https://www.e0575.cn/read.php?tid=11155105

http://www.sx.gov.cn/art/2010/4/19/art_1463100_16974304.html

https://baike. baidu. com/item/% E4%BD% 99%E7%85%8C/23318506? fr=

aladdin#3
https://baijiahao.baidu.com/s?id=1669086062260855353&wfr=spider&for=pc
https://baike. baidu. com/item/% E4%BD% 99%E6%99%8B% E5%92%8C/9708234?fr=aladdin
https://mp.weixin.qq.com/s/Jxqtd-30a5xzSL8jxKoPHQ
https://mp.weixin.qq.com/s/pNz7cy6k7uKq8lnEhTZ_Kg
http://www.zgkqw.com/zhuanti/system/2009/10/14/010138398.shtml
http://opinion.zjol.com.cn/rdht/201704/t20170421_3494733.shtml
https://baijiahao.baidu.com/s?id=1678220007546358897&wfr=spider&for=pc
https://www.sohu.com/a/386629851_770518
https://hzdaily.hangzhou.com.cn/dskb/page/3/2015-12/04/J10/20151204J10_pdf.pdf
http://www.360doc.com/content/18/1011/20/48619290_793934342.shtml
https://www.sohu.com/a/128184475_525464
https://kuaibao.qq.com/s/20200502A0FS8H00
http://news.fznews.com.cn/node/10269/20150810/55c868685e563.shtml

文化活动一：黄酒节

Cultural Activity (1): Yellow Rice Wine Festival

文化活动二：避暑胜地（一）

Cultural Activity (2): Summer Resort I

文化活动三：避暑胜地（二）

Cultural Activity (3): Summer Resort II

8月 August

文化活动一:黄酒节

Cultural Activity (1): Yellow Rice Wine Festival

文化寻踪之浙里村落 Ancient Towns

越城区东浦镇

Dongpu Town, Yuecheng District

浙江省绍兴市越城区的东浦镇素有"水乡、酒乡、桥乡、名士之乡"的美誉,是融江南水乡和黄酒文化的特色小镇。东浦是著名的水乡,河湖密布,水流纵横,有着最古老的水利工程之一;东浦是闻名于世的酒乡,是绍兴黄酒的发祥地,有1600余年的酿酒历史;东浦是独具魅力的桥乡,桥梁遍布,千姿百态,古朴典型,气势磅礴;东浦是群星璀璨的名士之乡,在这块古老的土地上孕育了不少政治家、革命家、军事家、科学家和文学家。

Located in Shaoxing City, Zhejiang Province, Dongpu Town is known as "water town, wine town, bridge town and the hometown of celebrities", and it is a characteristic town that integrates the charm of the south region of the Yangze River and the core of the rice wine culture. Dongpu is a famous water town with dense rivers and lakes, crisscrossing waters, and one of the oldest water conservancy projects; Dongpu is a world-famous wine town, the birthplace of Shaoxing rice wine, with a winemaking history of more than 1, 600 years; Dongpu is also the hometown of celebrities, and gave birth to many politicians, revolutionaries, military strategists, writers and scientists.

文化寻踪之浙里印记 Cultural Imprints

➢ 建筑文化 Architectural Culture

鲁东村泗龙桥 Silong Bridge in Ludong Village

泗龙桥位于浙江省绍兴市越城区东浦镇鲁东村，是青甸湖上的一条长虹，因桥形似龙卧在青甸湖水面上，桥上凿有4条龙而得名。泗龙桥由三孔石拱桥和十七孔石梁桥组成，全长96.4米，宽2米，南北向横跨，气势宏伟，景观秀美。该桥始建于宋朝，诗人陆游曾在其诗中多次题咏之。2013年3月，泗龙桥被国务院公布为全国重点文物保护单位。

The Silong Bridge is located in Ludong Village, Dongpu Town, Yuecheng District, Shaoxing City, Zhejiang Province. The bridge is shaped like a dragon lying on the Qingdian Lake, and there are four dragons carved on the bridge, hence its name the Silong Bridge, which means four dragons in sound. The bridge is composed of a three-hole stone arch bridge and a seventeen-hole stone beam bridge, with a total length of 96.4 meters and a width of 2 meters, spanning from north to south, with a magnificent momentum and beautiful landscape, just like rainbow on the Qingdian Lake. The bridge was first built in the Song Dynasty, and the poet Lu You once wrote it many times in his poems. In March 2013, the Silong Bridge was announced by the State Council as a national key cultural relics protection unit.

热诚学堂 Recheng School

热诚学堂,位于浙江省绍兴市镜湖新区东浦镇,今称东浦镇热诚小学。清光绪三十年(1904年),徐锡麟创办此校,以徐氏撰联"有热心人可与共学,具诚意者得入斯堂"取名。学堂提倡军训,实行男女同校。光绪三十三年(1907年),徐锡麟安庆起义失败,学堂一度受损。1915年,教学楼毁于大火,后以徐锡麟抚恤金重建。

Recheng School is located in Dongpu Town, Jinghu New District, Shaoxing City, Zhejiang Province. The school is now called Recheng Primary School of Dongpu Town. In the 13th year of Guangxu (1904) in the Qing Dynasty, Xu Xilin founded this school, named after Xu's couplet, "Enthusiastic people can learn together, and those who are sincere can enter the school". The school promoted military training and co-education. In the 33rd year of Guangxu (1907), the Anqing Uprising led by Xu Xilin failed and the school was once damaged. In 1915, the teaching building was destroyed by a fire and was later rebuilt with Xu's pension.

➢ 非遗文化
Intangible Cultural Heritage

绍兴黄酒酿制技艺Shaoxing Yellow Rice Wine Brewing Technique

绍兴黄酒酿制技艺源于春秋，成于北宋，兴于明清，传承流布于绍兴市及其周边区域，生产主要分布于鉴湖水系。绍兴黄酒是中国黄酒的杰出代表，一般为七月制酒药，九月制麦曲，十月制淋饭，大雪摊饭，次年立春时开始榨酒、煎酒，灌坛泥封后贮藏。经过千年演变和发展，绍兴黄酒酿制技艺不断改进和提高，已经成为中华民族宝贵的历史文化遗产，具有较高的学术、历史、艺术和良好的经济价值。

Shaoxing yellow rice wine brewing technique originated in the Spring and Autumn Period, developed in the Northern Song Dynasty, flourished in the Ming and Qing Dynasties, and spread in Shaoxing City and its surrounding areas. Shaoxing yellow rice wine is an outstanding representative of Chinese rice wine, and its production is mainly distributed in the Jianhu Lake area. Generally, the brewers begin to make Chinese yeast in the seventh lunar month; they make malt in the ninth lunar month; they make drenched rice in the tenth lunar month. Then they spread rice around Great Snow, that is, in December of the solar calendar. Onset the following spring the brewers begin to squeeze and boil wine, and then fill in the jars with the mouth sealed in mud. After thousands of years of evolution and development, Shaoxing yellow rice wine technique has been continuously improved, and it has become a precious historical and cultural heritage of the nation, with a high academic, historical, artistic and economic value.

➢ 名人文化
Celebrity Culture

徐锡麟 Xu Xilin

徐锡麟(1873—1907),字伯荪,号光汉子,清山阴东浦人。出身商人家庭,自幼秉性刚强,崇拜英雄豪杰。21岁中秀才,无意仕途,好论国事,曾任绍兴府中学堂教师并副监督,开设特别书局,经销新书,宣传革命。创办热诚学堂,自任体操教员。徐锡麟于1904年加入光复会,次年创办大通学堂,训练会党骨干,后捐道员官衔,去安徽任陆军小学堂会办、巡警学堂监督,以合法身份进行革命活动,准备浙皖起义。1907年5月26日,因事被察觉,仓促举义,枪杀巡抚恩铭,终因寡不敌众被捕,英勇捐躯。

Xu Xilin (1873-1907), courtesy name Guanghanzi, was born in a merchant family in Dongpu. He had a strong temperament and worshiped heroes since he was a child. At the age of 22, he got the title Xiucai (cultivated talent), a title bestowed on graduates of a certain examination in the state examination system. With no intention of following an official career but good at state affairs, he became a teacher and deputy supervisor of Shaoxing Middle School, opened a special bookstore, distributed new books, and promoted the revolution. He established Recheng School and became a gymnastics instructor. In 1904, he joined the Restoration Society, founded Datong School the following year, trained the backbone of the party, and later donated the official ranks of circuit intendant, and went to Anhui Province to serve as the Supervisor of the Army Primary School and the Patrol Academy, in preparation for Zhejiang and Anhui Uprising. On May 26, 1907, he was caught in a hasty act to shoot the provincial governor En Ming. As a result, he was arrested and died heroically.

文化寻踪之出行贴士 Travel Tips

寻踪之旅载体:黄酒节

寻踪之旅地点:浙江省绍兴市越城区东浦镇

寻踪之旅时间:8月

寻踪信息查询:(1)http://www.sxyc.gov.cn;(2)"绍兴旅游"微信公众平台;(3)搜狐、腾讯等多家网站。

Cultural Activity: Yellow Rice Wine Festival

Ancient Town: Dongpu Town, Yuecheng District, Shaoxing City, Zhejiang Province

Travel Time: August

For More Information: (1) Please visit http://www.sxyc.gov.cn; (2) Please search on the WeChat public platform "Shaoxing Lvyou"; (3) Please visit the websites such as Sohu, Tencent, etc.

参考资料

http://www.zjich.cn/news/newsshow.html?id=429969

http://www.bytravel.cn/Landscape/39/dongpuguzhen.html

http://www.tcmap.com.cn/zhejiangsheng/yuechengqu_dongpuzhen.html

http://www.bytravel.cn/landscape/109/rechengxuetangjiuzhi.html

https://baike. baidu. com/item/% E7%83%AD% E8%AF% 9A% E5%AD% A6%E5%A0%82

http://www.bytravel.cn/landscape/45/xuxiguju.html

http://www.sxyc.gov.cn/art/2018/12/17/art_1559713_27500155.html

http://www.zjich.cn/xiangmu/xiangmushow.html?id=194
https://zjnews.zjol.com.cn/system/2014/05/14/020024578.shtml
https://view.inews.qq.com/a/20200822A0OYIJ00
https://thewoksoflife.com/shaoxing-wine-the-key-to-authentic-chinese-cooking/
http://www.chinadaily.com.cn/food/2013-10/31/content_17070773_10.htm
http://culture.zjol.com.cn/05culture/system/2011/05/13/017517763.shtml
http://m.dianping.com/review/689701027

文化活动二:避暑胜地(一)

Cultural Activity (2): Summer Resort I

文化寻踪之浙里村落 Ancient Villages

➢ 武义县武阳镇郭洞村

Guodong Village, Wuyang Town, Wuyi County

郭洞村,位于距浙江武义县城10公里的群山幽岭之间,因山环如郭、幽邃如洞而得名。约5平方公里的景区内,层峦叠嶂,竹木苍翠,静雅宜人。"郭外风光凌北斗,洞中锦绣映南山",这是古人对郭洞风景区的贴切描绘。后代仿《内经图》营造村庄,砌城墙形成水口,建回龙桥聚气藏风,植村周树木善化环境,规划民居、通道并巧设七星井,形成绝佳的人居环境,被誉为"江南第一风水村"。

Located in Wuyi County, Zhejiang Province, 10 kilometers away from the downtown of the county, Guodong Village is surrounded by the mountains and ridges, and got the name "Guodong" because of its unique terrain, where the surrounding mountains are like city walls ("guo"), and the tranquil environment is like living in the caves ("dong"). In the scenic area of about 5 square kilometers, there are many cockroaches, bamboo and wood, quiet and elegant. The descendants constructed the village, imitating the treasure picture of "Inner Scripture" (Nei Jing Tu,《内经图》) from Baiyun Taoist Temple in Beijing. The village wall was built to form a water mouth, the Huilong Bridge was set up to gather the good Qi (good fortune), trees were planted around the village, the layout of residential buildings and passages were well planned, and a seven-star well was cleverly set up, all of which created the excellent living environment. Therefore, Guodong Village is known as the "No. 1 Fengshui village in the south of the Yangtze River".

文化寻踪之浙里印记 Cultural Imprints

➢ 建筑文化
Architectural Culture

何氏宗祠 He's Ancestral Hall

何氏宗祠建于明万历三十七年(1609),总面积1200平方米,规模宏大,气象庄严。这里是何家祭祀祖先的地方,何氏祖宗的牌位均立于此。祠堂内现在悬挂着30块匾额,据说最多时曾达94块。祠中还建有古朴典雅的古戏台和飞檐角,藻井上的壁画线条流畅,形象生动。

He's Ancestral Hall was built in the 37th year of Emperor Wanli (1609) of the Ming Dynasty, with a total area of 1,200 square meters, a grand scale and a majestic atmosphere. This is the place where the He family worships ancestors, and the memorial tablets of the He family's ancestors are all preserved here. There are now 30 plaques hanging in the ancestral hall, however, it is said that there were as many as 94 plaques in the past. There are also simple and elegant ancient stages and cornices in the hall, with the murals on caisson ceilings presenting smooth lines and vivid images.

新屋里 Xinwuli

新屋里是古民居的代表，三进共30间，气势不凡。它建于明崇祯年间，已有300多年的历史。8个窗子的木雕图案各不相同，正房窗雕百鸟绕庭和百鸟朝凤。西厢房雕喜鹊和百兽，配以产卵多的鱼虾，寄托子孙兴旺的愿望。东厢房窗子雕双狮耍球、鲤鱼跳龙门、松鼠等，表示依山水而居。围墙砖雕精美、图案丰富，有山水、人物故事、古钱币等。砌块组合精密，可以说现今不及。

Xinwuli is a representative of the ancient dwellings, with a total of 30 rooms in the three rows, which are all very spectacular. It was built in the reign of Emperor Chongzhen in the Ming Dynasty and has a history of more than 300 years. The woodcarving patterns of the eight windows are all different, with the windows of the main room carved with a hundred birds flying around the courtyard or paying homage to a phoenix, which implies birds become immortals as phoenixes. The windows of the west wing rooms are carved with magpies and wild beasts, accompanied by fish and shrimps, presenting the wishes of prosperous descendants. The windows of the east wing rooms are carved with two lions playing with balls, carps jumping on the dragon gate, and squirrels, etc., indicating that they live near the mountains and rivers. The brick walls are exquisitely carved and rich in patterns, including landscapes, character stories, and ancient coins, etc. The bricks on the wall were so tightly stacked that even today's construction technique may not be comparable.

熟溪桥 Shuxi Bridge

熟溪桥，位于熟溪河上。现存建筑系1946年按清乾隆时重建之原样修建。其为木石结构廊桥，南北走向，横跨熟溪。全长140米，桥面宽4.8米，通高13.4米。《光明日报》曾将熟溪桥称为“我国现存古代桥梁建筑中的艺术珍品”。如今，熟溪桥已成为武义的象征。

Situated on the Shuxi River, Wuyi County, the Shuxi Bridge is a wooden and stone covered bridge. This bridge was rebuilt in 1946 after the original shape which was once constructed during the Qianlong period of the Qing Dynasty. Going north-south and spanning the Shuxi River, the bridge is 140 meters in length, 4.8 meters in width, and 13.4 meters in height. *Guangming Daily*, one of the most influential newspapers in China, once called the Shuxi Bridge "an artistic treasure among the existing ancient bridges in China". Today, the Shuxi Bridge has become a symbol of Wuyi.

文化寻踪之出行贴士 Travel Tips

寻踪之旅载体:避暑胜地(一)

寻踪之旅地点:浙江省金华市武义县武阳镇郭洞村

寻踪之旅时间:通常为8月

寻踪信息查询:(1)http://www.zjwy.gov.cn/;(2)“武义旅游”微信公众平台;(3)搜狐、腾讯等多家网站。

Cultural Activity: Summer Resort I

Ancient Village: Guodong Village, Wuyang Town, Wuyi County, Jinhua City, Zhejiang Province

Travel Time: Usually in August

For More Information: (1) Please visit http://www.zjwy.gov.cn/; (2) Please search on the WeChat public platform “Wuyi Lvyou”; (3) Please visit the websites such as Sohu, Tencent, etc.

参考资料

http://travel.sina.com.cn/china/2014-12-02/1638287764_2.shtml

https://baike.so.com/doc/5617771-5830386.html

http://www.cchmi.com/tabid/95/InfoID/373/Default.aspx

https://lvyougl.com/lvyou/320675.html

http://www.forestry.gov.cn/main/72/20200122/164101707490854.html

http://www.guodongchina.com/about.htm

https://www.sohu.com/a/292757078_162323

https://www.sohu.com/a/325826623_162323

文化活动三:避暑胜地(二)

Cultural Activity (3): Summer Resort II

文化寻踪之浙里村落 Ancient Villages

➢ 婺城区汤溪镇寺平村

Siping Village, Tangxi Town, Wucheng District

寺平村坐落于浙江省金华市汤溪镇,毗邻九峰山。寺平村以戴姓为主,戴氏祖先从元末迁徙于此,繁衍至今已有700余年的历史。寺平村古厅堂众多,全村以"七星伴月"构建,即有七座依据七星方位建造的宏伟楼堂,具有徽派建筑风格。七座楼堂上应星宿、下合地势,中间围绕亘古皎洁的月湖,从而构成了寺平古村最为奇妙的自然人文景观。村中还时常有民俗展示,如茶艺、书法、竹编、茶罐窑等。

Siping Village is located in Tangxi Town, Jinhua City, Zhejiang Province, adjacent to Mountain Jiufeng. Dai is the dominating surname among the villagers, and it has been more than 700 years since the ancestors of the Dai family migrated here from the end of Yuan Dynasty. There are many ancient halls in Siping Village, and the construction layout is the "moon" accompanied by seven "stars". That is, the seven magnificent halls of Huizhou architectural style were arranged in the shape of the Big Dipper by the ancestors, in order to communicate harmony between the human and the natural world. There are folk custom displays in the village as well, such as tea art performance, calligraphy, bamboo weaving, tea pot kiln, etc., which have unique local characteristics.

文化寻踪之浙里印记 Cultural Imprints

➤ 建筑文化
Architectural Culture

砖雕民居 Residences with Brick Carving

清中期的寺平村特别流行砖雕艺术。这些砖雕或为戏剧人物,或为动物,或植物,或字,或风景,均栩栩如生。"九狮戏球"和"鲤鱼跳龙门"是寺平村最具代表性的大型砖雕作品,浮雕、圆雕和透雕的技法细腻,造型栩栩如生、凌空欲动。在这些砖雕艺术中有徽派的痕迹,但是同徽派砖雕最大的不同是寺平的砖雕是生雕,即雕刻好再烧,技术难度非常高。其中百顺堂、崇厚堂、立本堂、基顺堂等建筑,气势恢宏,砖雕作品精美灵动,因此也被誉为"中国最漂亮的砖雕民居"。

In the middle of the Qing Dynasty, the art of brick carving was especially popular in Siping Village. These bricks usually vividly depict drama figures, animals, plants, characters and landscape, etc., among which "Nine Lions Scrambling for a Ball" and "Carps Jumping over the Dragon Gate" are the most representative large-scale brick carving works. The technique of relief carving, circular carving and penetrative carving was skillfully employed, and each work was delicate and lifelike. There are traces of Huizhou style in these brick carvings, but the biggest difference between the two schools is that these brick carvings in Siping are raw carvings, that is, they are carved and then fired, whose technique is more difficult. Among them, the ancient buildings such as Baishun Hall, Chonghou Hall, Liben Hall, Jishun Hall, etc., are magnificent, and their brick carvings are exquisite. Therefore, they are also known as "the residences with the most beautiful brick carvings in China".

文化寻踪之出行贴士 Travel Tips

寻踪之旅载体:避暑胜地(二)

寻踪之旅地点:浙江省金华市婺城区汤溪镇寺平村

寻踪之旅时间:通常为8月

寻踪信息查询:(1)http://www.wuch.gov.cn;(2)"金华旅游"微信公众平台;(3)搜狐、腾讯等多家网站。

Cultural Activity: Summer Resort II

Ancient Town: Siping Village, Tangxi Town, Wucheng District, Jinhua City, Zhejiang Province

Travel Time: Usually in August

For More Information: (1) Please visit http://www.wuch.gov.cn; (2) Please search on the WeChat public platform "Jinhua Lvyou"; (3) Please visit the websites such as Sohu, Tencent, etc.

参考资料

https://zjnews.zjol.com.cn/05zjnews/system/2012/03/31/018378531.shtml

http://www.jinhua.gov.cn/art/2015/2/2/art_1229159975_50267326.html

http://www.jinhua.gov.cn/art/2013/11/5/art_1229159934_50250003.html

https://www.sohu.com/a/126947849_451577

http://jhwcw.zjol.com.cn/wcnews/system/2013/05/31/016493938.shtml

http://wxzx.zjol.com.cn/11wxzx/system/2017/09/03/021588016.shtml

https://xw.qq.com/cmsid/20200225A00BPJ00?f=newdc

http://jhwcw.zjol.com.cn/wcnews/system/2019/10/30/031994142.shtml

http://jinhua.zjol.com.cn/jinhua/system/2014/05/08/017964159.shtml?&from=androidqq

http://www.jinhua-homestay.com/en/siping.php

文化寻踪之推荐日历
Recommended Month

9月 September

文化活动（一）：九月初一庙会
Cultural Activity (1): Temple Fair on the First Day of the Ninth Lunar Month

文化活动（二）：观潮节
Cultural Activity (2): Tidal Bore Watching Festival

文化活动（三）：南浔区菱湖镇菱文化节
Cultural Activity (3): Water Caltrop Cultural Festival in Linghu Town, Nanxun District

文化活动（四）：南浔区双林镇菱文化节
Cultural Activity (4): Water Caltrop Cultural Festival in Shuanglin Town, Nanxun District

文化活动（五）：庆元菇神庙会
Cultural Activity (5): Mushroom God Temple Fair in Qingyuan

文化活动（六）：赏桂花和红枫等特色树木
Cultural Activity (6): Appreciating the Characteristic Trees Such as Osmanthus and Red Maples

文化活动一:九月初一庙会

Cultural Activity (1):

Temple Fair on the First Day of the Ninth Lunar Month

文化寻踪之浙里村落 Ancient Towns

➢ 富阳区龙门镇

Longmen Town, Fuyang District

位于富春江南岸的龙门镇,是个距杭州市区仅38公里的小镇。这里是三国东吴开国皇帝孙权的故里。龙门镇以独特的明、清古建筑群而闻名,是现今江南地区明清古建筑群中保存较为完整的山乡古镇。全镇四面皆山,山势南高北低,是一个小盆地。龙门山崛起于东南端,大头山盘踞于西南一隅。龙门山主峰杏梅尖海拔1067.6米,为本市最高峰。

Longmen, the ancient town of the south bank of the Fuchun River, is a small town where is only 38 kilometers away from downtown Hangzhou. This is the hometown of Sun Quan, the Great Emperor of the Three

Kingdoms (namely Wei, Shu Han and Wu). Longmen Town is well-known for its unique Ming and Qing architectural complex and it is a relatively well-preserved mountainous ancient town in the south of the Yangtze River. The surrounding mountains are high in the south and low in the north, forming a small basin. With an altitude of 1067.6 meters, Xingmeijian, the main peak of Longmen Mountain, is the highest one in the city.

文化寻踪之浙里印记 Cultural Imprints

➢ 建筑文化 Architectural Culture

龙门古建筑群 Longmen Ancient Architectural Complex

龙门古建筑群位于杭州市富阳区龙门镇,年代为明至民国。古镇背靠龙门山,北依剡溪,龙门溪穿村而过。山水之间留下的是现今江南地区保存最为完整的明清古建筑群之一,亦被誉为“江南古镇活化石”。龙门镇居民以孙姓居多,是三国东吴大帝孙权家族的后裔,这里也是孙权后裔的最大聚居地。千百年来,经一代又一代的建筑,从一个大家庭的聚居地,形成了今日的古镇。古镇建筑以两座孙氏宗祠为中心,共建有四十多座孙氏厅堂、三座砖砌牌楼、一座古塔和一座寺庙。镇内屋舍房廊相连,长街曲巷连贯相通,镇外的人进入镇里,如入迷宫。

Longmen ancient architectural complex is located in Longmen Town, Fuyang District, Hangzhou City, dating from the Ming Dynasty to the Republic of China. The ancient town is backed to Mountain Longmen, and close to the Shan Stream in the north, with the Longmen Stream running through the village. Longmen Town is one of the most well-preserved ancient architectural complexes, and it also gets the fame of the "living fossil of the ancient town in the south of the Yangtze River". Most residents in Longmen Town are surnamed Sun, who are known as the descendants of the family of Sun Quan, the Great Emperor of the Three Kingdoms. Therefore, this is also the largest habitation of Sun Quan's descendants. After thousands of years, today's ancient town has been gradually formed from a large family settlement through generations' efforts. The ancient town's architecture is centered on two Sun's ancestral halls. There are more than forty Sun's halls, three brick decorated archways, one ancient tower and one temple. The houses and rooms in the town are connected by corridors and long streets. Visitors entering here are like entering a maze.

非遗文化
Intangible Cultural Heritage

龙门九月初一庙会 Longmen Temple Fair on the First Day of the Ninth Lunar Month

龙门九月初一庙会是杭州市富阳龙门镇的传统庙会。庙会的起源最早可追溯到北宋年间，是民俗文化的"活标本"，集中展示了富有江南特色的民俗传统。相传龙门孙氏后裔为纪念祖先孙钟的功德而建了"荫功天子庙"，选定九月初一开庙，庙会风俗由此延续至今。庙会期间，龙门镇会举行祭祀先祖、办宴席、做善事、开社戏等各类活动。族人遍邀亲朋好友，倾其所有，热情招待，方圆百里的商贩也会纷纷前来赶会。目前龙门庙会仍是富春江两岸最热闹的节庆活动，已经成为龙门旅游景区民俗文化活动的重要内容。

Longmen Temple Fair on the first day of the ninth lunar month is a traditional temple fair in Longmen Ancient Town, Fuyang District, Hangzhou. The origin of the temple fair can be traced back to the Northern Song Dynasty. It is regarded as a living specimen of folk culture that intensively displays the folk traditions with characteristics of the south of the Yangtze River. Legend has it that, the descendants of the Longmen Sun family built the temple in order to commemorate their ancestor Sun Zhong, whose grandson became the emperor due to his good conduct. The fair was scheduled to start on the first day of the ninth lunar month, and the custom continues to this day. During the temple fair, various folk activities will be held such as offering sacrifices to ancestors, hosting banquets, doing good deeds, and holding village operas, etc. Relatives and friends will be invited and traders from all over the area will come to join the fair. Nowadays Longmen Temple Fair is still the most boisterous event on both sides of the Fuchun River, and it has become an important part of the folk cultural activities in the Longmen Scenic Area.

文化寻踪之出行贴士 Travel Tips

寻踪之旅载体:九月初一庙会

寻踪之旅地点:浙江省杭州市富阳区龙门镇

寻踪之旅时间:通常为9月

寻踪信息查询:(1)https://hangzhou.zjol.com.cn;(2)“杭州龙门古镇”微信公众平台;(3)搜狐、腾讯等多家网站。

Cultural Activity: Temple Fair on the First Day of the Ninth Lunar Month

Ancient Town: Longmen Town, Fuyang District, Hangzhou City,

Zhejiang Province

Travel Time: Usually in September

For More Information: (1) Please visit https://hangzhou.zjol.com.cn; (2) Please search on the WeChat public platform “Hangzhou Longmen Guzhen”; (3) Please visit the websites such as Sohu, Tencent, etc.

参考资料

https://hangzhou.zjol.com.cn/jrsd/bwzg/202007/t20200707_12115164.shtml

https://baike. baidu. com/item/% E9%BE% 99%E9%97%A8%E9%95%87/4844613

http://www.tcmap.com.cn/zhejiangsheng/fuyang_longmenzhen.html

http://www.zjich.cn/xiangmu/xiangmushow.html?id=1453

http://www.huaxia.com/ly/lyzx/2012/10/3036528.html

https://baijiahao.baidu.com/s?id=1669740116589046718&wfr=spider&for=pc

https://baike. baidu. com/item/% E6%9D% AD% E5%B7%9E% E9%BE%99%E9%97%A8%E5%8F%A4%E9%95%87/5846059?fr=aladdin

https://www.sohu.com/a/37447223_271067

https://baijiahao.baidu.com/s?id=1612636285682811145&wfr=spider&for=pc

文化活动二：观潮节

Cultural Activity (2): Tidal Bore Watching Festival

文化寻踪之浙里村落 Ancient Towns

➢ 海宁市盐官镇
Yanguan Town, Haining City

海宁市盐官镇位于中国长江三角洲的南端，是良渚文化的一大重要发源地，也是吴越文化的交汇地，因从汉代开始晒盐制盐而闻名。盐官是中国唯一的潮乡，地处钱塘江强潮地段，优越的地理位置使其成为天下奇观钱江潮的最佳观赏地。盐官镇工业发展以电子信息和五金机电两大产业为支柱，是国家火炬计划软磁材料产业基地和小五金生产基地。盐官镇农业发展具有鲜明产业特色，以大棚蔬菜和行道树苗木生产为主导产业，被誉为“中国行道树第一镇”。

Situated in the southern end of the Yangtze River Delta in China,

Yanguan Town, Haining City is an important birthplace of Liangzhu culture and the intersection of Wu and Yue regional culture. It has been famous for its salt making and drying industry since the Han Dynasty. Yanguan is the only tidal town which is located in the mighty tidal bore area of the Qiantang River in China. Its superior geographical location makes it the best place to watch the Qianjiang tide, which is known as the wonder of the world. The electronic information industry and the hardware and electrical industry have become the two main industries of Yanguan town, which boast the national Torch Plan soft magnetic materials industry base and hardware production base. The agricultural development of Yanguan has distinctive features. With the production of greenhouse vegetables and street tree seedlings as its leading industries, it is known as the "No. 1 town of street trees in China".

文化寻踪之浙里印记 Cultural Imprints

建筑文化 Architectural Culture

鱼鳞石塘(钱塘江海塘)Fish Scale Seawall (Qiantang River Seawall)

鱼鳞石塘(钱塘江海塘)被誉为"捍海长城",是人类改造自然的伟大成果,是中国最伟大的建筑工程和科技文化遗产之一。鱼鳞石塘于中国的清代初期开始修建,修筑方法十分特别,全部用整齐的长方形条石丁顺上迭,自下而上顺次叠砌。每块条石之间用糯米浆砌筑,再用铁锔扣榫,并加帮土墩护塘。其背水处则以地壅固加厚,并形成地堰,工程浩大。从侧面看塘身,层次排列如同鱼鳞,整齐美观且坚固,因此得名"鱼鳞石塘"。

The fish scale Seawall is known as the "Great Wall to defend the sea". It is a great achievement of mankind's transformation of nature and one of China's greatest architectural projects and cultural heritages of science and technology. The fish scale seawall was first built in the early Qing Dynasty, and the construction method was very special. All the neat rectangular stones were stacked up from bottom to the top layer by layer, and the glutinous rice paste was plastered between the layers to seal the structure. The iron was used to buckle the tenon, and the mounds were placed for added strength. The back surface was thickened with ground solidification and formed a ground weir, which was a huge project. Viewed from the side, the layout was like fish scale, neat and solid, hence the name "fish scale seawall".

宰相府第风情街 Style Street

宰相府第风情街位于海宁盐官古城,是一条以清代宰相府第陈阁老宅为主景的古街。街区融官僚豪宅、名人故居、城隍古庙、传统商铺、特色民居于一体,古风悠悠,风情独特。街区由四大区块组成:城楼区块、茶楼区块、人文区块和邑庙区块。它是一条既蕴含着深厚的历史文化又再现了江南古城风情的特色人文街。

The style street, where the former residence of Chen Yuanlong (the cabinet minister in the Qing Dynasty) is located, is situated in the ancient city of Yanguan, Haining. The block integrates bureaucratic mansions, former residences of celebrities, ancient temples, traditional shops, and characteristic residential houses, with a long and unique style. The street consists of four major blocks, namely the watchtower block, the tea house block, the humanity culture block and the city god temple block. It is a characteristic humanistic street that not only contains a profound history and culture, but also reproduces the amorous feelings of an ancient city in the south of the Yangtze River.

海神庙 Temple of the Sea God

海神庙又称庙宫,是江南地区最大的敕建官式建筑遗存之一,石雕精美,具有重要的文化和艺术价值,充分显示了古代工匠精湛的工艺技巧和完美的艺术造型。其结构仿故宫太和殿,故也有“银銮殿”之称。海神庙是祭祀传说中的“浙海之神”,正殿中设一无名之神,钱镠、伍子胥享配左右。全庙共分九院,均为清朝宫殿式建筑。

Temple of the sea god, also known as Temple Palace, is one of the largest relics of official-style buildings in the south of the Yangtze River. The stone carvings are exquisite and have an important cultural and artistic value, which fully demonstrates the exquisite craftsmanship and perfect artistic modeling of ancient craftsmen, and its structure resembles the Hall of Supreme Harmony in the Forbidden City. Since the temple was to worship the legendary sea god, an unnamed god was built in the main hall, while the founding monarch of Wu and Yue named Qian Liu and the military strategist at the end of the Spring and Autumn Period named Wu Zixu, stand on the left and right sides respectively. The whole temple is divided into nine halls, all of which are palace-style buildings in the Qing Dynasty.

安国寺经幢 Stone Columns with Buddhist Scriptures in Anguo Temple

安国寺经幢是海宁市全国重点文物保护单位，三座经幢平面均呈八角形，形态优美，冠于浙江，是艺术价值相当高的珍贵文物。座身镌刻图案，腰檐仿木构建筑，是中国最早出现的石构仿木经幢。整个经幢亭亭玉立，层次丰富，典雅美观，是研究中国南方唐代建筑极为难得的实物例证。

The stone columns with Buddhist scripture in Anguo Temple are major national-level protected historical and cultural sites in Haining City. Octagonal in plane and beautiful in shape, the three stone columns with Buddhist scriptures enjoy a great popularity in Zhejiang and are regarded as precious cultural relics with a high artistic value. The columns, with elegant patterns and designs modeled after wood construction, are the earliest ones with Buddhist scriptures which imitated wood structure in China, and they are rare physical examples for studying the architecture of the Tang Dynasty in southern China.

非遗文化
Intangible Cultural Heritage

海宁皮影戏 Haining Shadow Play

一块白色幕布，艺人们在布后，一边操纵影偶，一边用本土曲调讲述故事，配上打击乐和弦乐，一出传统的皮影戏便开场了。皮影戏起源于西汉，道具主要为影窗，以白纸作幕，其次为油灯一盏，用以映射影人和表演动作，是民间工艺美术与传统戏曲巧妙结合，并融入了戏剧、音乐等多种

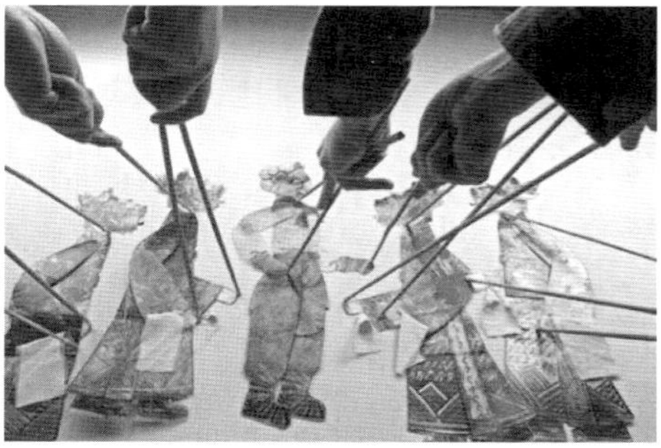

艺术手段的古老戏曲艺术品种，是中国古老而精美的傀儡戏。海宁皮影是江南皮影的代表，具有典型的南宋风格。海宁皮影戏的唱腔运用了“海盐腔”和“弋阳腔”，并夹杂着地方戏曲以及山歌调、采茶调等民间小调，极富水乡韵味。

A white screen, some artists, some percussion instruments, and stringed instruments, and a few flat puppets that can move and tell a story compose shadow play. Shadow play originated in the Western Han Dynasty, and the main props were shadow windows, with white paper as the backdrop, illuminated by an oil lamp, which were used to project the puppet figures and perform actions. The ancient shadow puppetry has now formed an artistic combination of opera, music, fine art and special craftsmanship. Haining shadow play is a representative of shadow puppets in the south of the Yangtze River, presenting a typical Southern Song style. Haining shadow play formed its unique style by using tunes from Yiyang and Haiyan, mixed with local opera, folk songs and tea-picking tunes, which are full of charms of a watery town.

海宁观潮 Haining Tidal Bore Watching

海宁潮是一个壮观无比的自然动态奇观。杭州湾至钱塘江口外宽内窄，呈喇叭口状，出海口宽度达100公里，江潮以每秒10米的流速向前推进。此时涌潮受到两岸急剧收缩的影响，水体涌积，夺路叠进，潮波不断增高，潮头便形如立墙，势若冲天，举世闻名的海宁潮便由此形成。当江潮从东涌来时，似一条银线，渐渐地，滔天浊浪，轰响如雷，有吞天沃日之势，雄伟壮丽，惊心动魄。

The tidal bore in Haining is a spectacular dynamic natural wonder. The river section from Hangzhou Bay to the Qiantang River estuary is wide outside and narrow inside. With a trumpet-like shape, the estuary is 100 kilometers wide, and the tidal bore can advance at a speed of 10 meters per second. At this point, the tide flowing out was influenced by a sharp contraction of the two sides. As a result, the mighty waves surge increasingly. As it reaches Yanguan Town, it evolves into a one-line tidal bore, attracting so many visitors to gather and take a glimpse of the power of nature.

名人文化
Celebrity Culture

王国维故居 The Former Residence of Wang Guowei

王国维故居坐落于盐官镇，是木结构庭院式民居。粉墙黛瓦的王国维故居有着江南水乡独特的古建筑风格。故居共二进，前进为平屋，三开间，后进为楼房，两进之间有天井及两厢，整组建筑自成独立院落。1886年，其父王乃誉将全家从城内双仁巷搬迁至此，取名为“娱庐”，王国维称其为“西城老屋”。王国维在此度过了青少年时代的12个春秋，后来虽游学在外，仍多次回此小住。

The former residence of Wang Guowei is located in Yanguan Town and it is a wooden courtyard house. With white walls and black tiles, the residence has a unique ancient architectural style that is a typical watery town in the south of the Yangtze River. There are two rows of constructions in the residence. The front row is a bungalow with three rooms, while the back row is a building, and there is a courtyard and wing rooms between the two rows. The whole complex is being considered as an enclosed house. In 1886, his father Wang Naiyu, moved his family from Shuangren Alley in the city to this place and named it "Yu Cottage". Wang Guowei called it the "Old House in Xicheng", and he spent 12 teenage years here. Later, even though he studied abroad, he still returned to live here many times.

文化寻踪之出行贴士 Travel Tips

寻踪之旅载体:观潮节

寻踪之旅地点:浙江省海宁市盐官镇

寻踪之旅时间:9月

寻踪信息查询:(1)http://www.haining.gov.cn;(2)"诗画浙江48小时"微信公众平台;(3)搜狐、腾讯等多家网站。

Cultural Activity: Tidal Bore Watching Festival

Ancient Town: Yanguan Town, Haining City, Zhejiang Province

Travel Time: September

For More Information: (1) Please visit http://www.haining.gov.cn; (2) Please search on the WeChat public platform "Shihua Zhejiang 48 Xiaoshi"; (3) Please visit the websites such as Sohu, Tencent, etc.

参考资料

http://www.haining.gov.cn/art/2020/4/30/art_1229285380_130234.html

https://mp.weixin.qq.com/s/sXiBsT9qqFWuabaDInQrrQ

http://www.qianjiangchao.com/gcj/8.htm

http://www. zjzwfw. gov. cn/zjservice/street/list/streetinfo. do? adcode=330481110000&webid=1063&name=

http://hnnews.zjol.com.cn/hnnews/system/2010/07/26/012425686.shtml

http://www.jiaxing.gov.cn/art/2013/12/11/art_1536136_21860655.html

https://m.sohu.com/a/274441367_220858

http://www.jiaxing.gov.cn/art/2015/12/16/art_1592462_26792114.html

http://jiaxing.lvyou114.com/jingdian/zaixiangfudifengqingjie/profile

https://baike.baidu.com/item/%E5%AE%B0%E7%9B%B8%E5%BA%9C%E7%AC% AC% E9%A3%8E% E6%83%85%E8%A1%97/4312050? fr=aladdin

http://www.jiaxing.gov.cn/art/2017/6/15/art_1536136_21861057.html

https://m.sohu.com/a/431602208_823812

http://www.jiaxing.gov.cn/art/2014/1/13/art_1536216_22023117.html

https://www.sohu.com/a/255417967_399486

http://www.jiaxing.gov.cn/art/2014/1/13/art_1536216_22023099.html

http://www.jiaxing.gov.cn/art/2019/10/18/art_1578779_38978820.html

https://baike.baidu.com/item/%E5%AE%89%E5%9B%BD%E5%AF%BA%E7%BB%8F%E5%B9%A2/8797176?fr=aladdin

http://wap.bytravel.cn/landscape/22/anguosijingchuang.html

http://www.ihchina.cn/Article/Index/detail?id=18624

http://www.ihchina.cn/Article/Index/detail?id=10162

http://www.ihchina.cn/Article/Index/detail?id=10652

http://www.ihchina.cn/Article/Index/detail?id=13397

http://www.jiaxing.gov.cn/art/2018/4/23/art_1536139_21860406.html

http://www.jiaxing.gov.cn/art/2008/10/27/art_1536140_21860037.html

http://jx.zjol.com.cn/system/2016/09/01/021284565.shtml

https://m.sohu.com/a/140895339_217906

http://www.jiaxing.gov.cn/art/2014/1/13/art_1536216_22023100.html

https://global.chinadaily.com.cn/a/202101/23/WS600b8563a31024ad0baa4951_5.html

https://www.shine.cn/feature/art-culture/2003265092/

http://travel.qunar.com/travelbook/note/7394318

https://www.shine.cn/feature/art-culture/1901318974/

http://subsites.chinadaily.com.cn/ezhejiang/2016-08/12/c_55749.htm

http://en.hubei.gov.cn/culture/intangible/201306/t20130627_455890.shtml

文化活动三:南浔区菱湖镇菱文化节

Cultural Activity (3): Water Caltrop Cultural Festival in Linghu Town, Nanxun District

文化寻踪之浙里村落 Ancient Towns

➢ 南浔区菱湖镇

Linghu Town, Nanxun District

菱湖镇古时是被用来种菱的大湖。每年秋季大片菱叶随波飘扬,朵朵菱花背着太阳盛开,因名"菱湖"。早在唐宝历元年(825),湖州刺史崔元亮修建凌波塘,建造秀溪桥,因此"秀溪"和"凌波塘"为此镇的别名。菱湖水产丰富,商人聚集,是以被称为水市,逐步形成集镇。

Linghu Town was originally a large lake, which was used for growing water caltrops in the ancient times. Every autumn, a large piece of water caltrop leaves fluttering with the waves, and blossoming water caltrop flowers bloom with their backs to the sun, hence it was named as the

Linghu Lake (Water Caltrop Lake). As early as the first year of Baoli (825) in the Tang Dynasty, Huzhou governor Cui Yuanliang built the Lingbo Pond and the Xiuxi Bridge, hence the two other names "Lingbo Pond" and "Xiuxi" for the town. Rich in aquatic products, Linghu Town came to prominence due to the flourishing merchandising and has been reputed as a water market.

文化寻踪之浙里印记 Cultural Imprints

➢ 建筑文化 Architectural Culture

菱湖安澜桥 Linghu Anlan Bridge

安澜桥，位于浙江省湖州市菱湖镇，是湖州重要建筑文物之一。该桥未建前，湖西墩与菱湖镇靠南北渡船交通。由于湖面较宽，有时风浪很大，百姓来往十分危险。清乾隆四十二年，在同乡人协力捐资下，安澜桥最终建成。1949年后，该桥随着镇、乡、村经济建设的发展，已成为菱湖镇西北郊水陆路的交通重要通道。

The Anlan Bridge, located in Linghu Town, Huzhou City, Zhejiang Province, is one of the important architectural cultural relics in Huzhou. Before the bridge was built, the transportation between west pier of the lake and Linghu Town were north-south ferries. Since the lake was wide and the wind and waves were very strong at times, it was dangerous for local people to take a boat. In the 42nd year of Emperor Qianlong of the

Qing Dynasty, the Anlan Bridge was finally built with the donated funding from the fellow villagers. After 1949, with the development of economic construction in towns, townships, and villages, the bridge has become an important transportation center for Linghu to suppress water and land routes in the northwestern suburbs.

➢ 非遗文化
Intangible Cultural Heritage

震远同茶食“三珍”制作技艺 Zhenyuantong Tea Food Making Technique

湖州震远同,是一个在华东地区享有盛誉的百年老字号。有吴兴茶食“三珍”美称的玫瑰酥糖、椒盐桃片、牛皮糖是震远同的主要产品,以其独特的传统制作工艺和口味赢得了广大消费者的青睐,蕴含着湖州地区古老而富有特色的传统食品文化。

Huzhou Zhenyuantong is a century-old brand with a high reputation in East China. Zhenyuantong's main products include rose crisp candy, salt and pepper peach slices, and cowhide candy, which are reputed as the “three treasures” of Wuxing tea food. They have won the attention from consumers with their unique traditional production technique and taste, representing a distinctive traditional food culture of Huzhou.

射中村与后羿神话 The Myth of Hou Yi and Shezhong Village

位于菱湖镇的射中村,古时名为射村,起源于后羿射九日的神话传说。村中建有羿神庙,是供奉后羿和嫦娥神像的地方,有祭祀后羿、嫦娥的民俗。后羿射日与嫦娥奔月的相关故事在射中村代代相传,妇孺皆知。

Shezhong Village, located in Linghu Town, was named She Village in ancient times and originated from the myth of Hou Yi shooting down nine suns. There is a temple of God Hou Yi, which is a place to worship Hou Yi and Chang'e. There are also folk customs to pay tribute to Hou Yi and Chang'e. The fairy tales about Hou Yi's shooting down nine suns and Chang'e flying to the moon have been passed down from generation to generation in the village, and almost known by everyone.

➢ 名人文化 Celebrity Culture

竹墩"三沈" The Three Shens of Zhudun Village

竹墩"三沈"指曾于20世纪20年代同时任教于北京大学的三兄弟沈士远、沈尹默、沈兼士,祖籍为南浔区菱湖镇竹墩村,均为北京大学文科教授。其中,沈士远是研究庄子的专家,沈尹默是著名的学者、诗人、教育家和书法家,沈兼士是著名的语言文字学家和文献档案学家。三兄弟均为中国文化发展做出了杰出贡献。

The Three Shens of Zhudun refer to the three brothers—Shen Shiyuan, Shen Yinmo, and Shen Jianshi who taught at Peking University in the 1920s, and whose ancestral home is Zhudun Village, Linghu Town, Nanxun District. They all became professors of liberal arts at Peking University. Among them, Shen Shiyuan was an expert on Zhuangzi; Shen Yinmo was a famous scholar, poet, educator and calligrapher; and Shen Jianshi was a famous linguistic philologist and documentary archivist. All three brothers made outstanding contributions to the development of Chinese culture.

文化寻踪之出行贴士 Travel Tips

寻踪之旅载体:南浔区菱湖镇菱文化节

寻踪之旅地点:浙江省湖州市南浔区菱湖镇

寻踪之旅时间:通常为9月中下旬

寻踪信息查询:(1)http://www.nanxun.gov.cn;(2)"南浔旅游"微信公众平台;(3)搜狐、腾讯等多家网站。

Cultural Activity: Water Caltrop Cultural Festival in Linghu Town, Nanxun District

Ancient Town: Linghu Town, Nanxun District, Huzhou City, Zhejiang Province

Travel Time: Usually in mid to late September

For More Information: (1) Please visit http://www.nanxun.gov.cn; (2) Please search on the WeChat public platform "Nanxun Lvyou"; (3) Please visit the websites such as Sohu, Tencent, etc.

参考资料

http://www.zjich.cn/xiangmu/xiangmushow.html?id=1092

http://www.zjich.cn/xiangmu/xiangmushow.html?id=924

https://www.sohu.com/a/231486074_790623

http://en.chinaculture.org/chineseway/2013-07/10/content_467182_4.htm

https://www.chinahighlights.com/hangzhou/attraction/nanxun-town.htm

https://www.sohu.com/a/416956058_434584

http://www.huzhou.gov.cn/col/col1229213975/index.html

http://en.chinaculture.org/info/2013-09/17/content_484622.htm

http://www.hyzx.gov.cn/wszl/ssyj/1690.html

http://www.hyxw.com.cn/Article/mtgz/qtmt/201412/10101.html

https://town.zjol.com.cn/zxz/201806/t20180604_7464284.shtml

https://zjnews.zjol.com.cn/zjnews/huzhounews/201810/t20181019_8517087.shtml

文化活动四：南浔区双林镇菱文化节

Cultural Activity (4):

Water Caltrop Cultural Festival in Shuanglin Town, Nanxun District

文化寻踪之浙里村落 Ancient Towns

➢ 南浔区双林镇

Shuanglin Town, Nanxun District

双林镇位于湖州市南浔区，是一座历史悠久的江南名镇。据对附近洪城、花城等古文化遗址的发掘研究，早在四千年前就有先民在此居住。到了汉唐，这里变成了一个叫东林的村庄。南宋时，北方商人随宋室南迁于此，故又称商林。明永乐三年(1405)，与邻近的西林村合并，改名双林镇，沿用至今。

Shuanglin Town, located in Nanxun District, Huzhou City, is a famous town in the south of the Yangtze River with a long history. According to the research of ancient cultural sites such as Hongcheng and

Huacheng nearby, ancestors lived here as early as four thousand years ago. In the Han and Tang Dynasties, it became a village called Donglin. In the Southern Song Dynasty, northern merchants moved south with the royal family of the Southern Song Dynasty, so it was also called as Shanglin ("Shang" refers to merchants). In the third year of Emperor Yongle (1405) in the Ming Dynasty, it merged with Xilin Village nearby, and was renamed Shuanglin Town, which is still in use today.

文化寻踪之浙里印记 Cultural Imprints

建筑文化
Architectural Culture

双林三桥 Shuanglin Tri-bridges

双林三桥位于浙江省湖州市双林镇,为湖州东南部胜景之一。双林三桥是第七批全国重点文物保护单位,往来船只距镇数里即可望见横跨在河上的三座桥:万元桥、化成桥和万魁桥。

Situated in Shuanglin Town, Huzhou City, Zhejiang Province, the Shuanglin Tri-bridges are one of the scenic spots in southeast Huzhou, and the seventh batch of major national-level protected historical and cultural sites. The three bridges, the Wanyuan Bridge, the Huacheng Bridge, and the Wankui Bridge across the river can be seen a few kilometers away from the town on the ships passing by.

幻溇古桥群 Huanlou Ancient Bridge Group

幻溇古桥群是浙江省的重点文物保护单位，是双林镇一处著名的古桥胜景。它由三座古桥组成，分别是永安桥、明溪塘桥和埭溪塘桥。永安桥建于清道光年间，位于双林镇的千亩山行政村；后两座建于民国时期，位于双林镇的镇西乡土山行政村。

The Huanlou ancient bridge group is a historical and cultural site protected at the municipal level in Zhejiang Province. It is a famous scenic spot in Shuanglin Town, composed of three ancient bridges, namely the Yong'an Bridge, the Mingxitang Bridge and the Daixitang Bridge. The Yong'an Bridge was built in the reign of Emperor Daoguang of the Qing Dynasty and located in Qianmushan Administrative Village of Shuanglin Town, while the latter two were built at the Republic of China and located in Tushan Administrative Village of Zhenxi Township, Shuanglin Town.

➢ 非遗文化
Intangible Cultural Heritage

双林绫绢织造技艺 Shuanglin Silk Damask Weaving Technique

双林绫绢织造技艺是湖州南浔区双林镇的传统手工艺。绫绢是绫与绢的合称，以复杂装饰图案的丝绸为绫，而纯色丝绸为绢。绫绢于2008年被列入第二批国家代表性非物质文化遗产名录。双林绫绢的传统织造技艺历史悠久。根据相关文献和历史记载，早在东晋时期，吴兴太守王献之已用白色绢丝书写。到了宋朝，双林绫绢举世闻名，并出口到越南、柬埔寨、印度和斯里兰卡等十多个东南亚国家。根据吴兴县志，织造技术在明代得到了进一步发展。

Shuanglin silk damask weaving technique is a traditional handicraft in Shuanglin Town, Nanxun District, Huzhou. Silk damask is a general term for damask silk and spun silk. The silk with complex decorative patterns is damask silk and that with plain colors is spun silk. Silk damask was listed in the second catalogue of national representative intangible cultural heritages in 2008. The traditional weaving technique of Shuanglin silk damask has a long history. Related literature and historical records stated that, Wang Xianzhi, prefecture chief of Wuxing in feudal China had already used spun silk to write in the Eastern Jin Dynasty. Shuanglin silk damask was famous in the world in the Song Dynasty, and was exported to more than ten Southeast Asian countries such as Vietnam, Cambodia, India and Sri Lanka. According to Wuxing County's records, the weaving technique was developed further in the Ming Dynasty.

湖剧 Huzhou Opera

湖剧，是浙北地区唯一具有代表性的地方戏曲剧种，旧称湖州滩簧，曾被称为“小戏”“花鼓”“湖州文戏”。流行于浙北的湖州、嘉兴各县，以及江苏吴江、宜兴等地。湖剧的发展大致经历了小戏时期、本滩时期和剧本戏时期三个时期。

Huzhou opera is the only representative local opera genre in northern Zhejiang. It was formerly known as Huzhou Tanhuang drama and was once known as "Little Opera", "Flower-Drum" and "Huzhou Gentle Drama". It is popular in Huzhou and Jiaxing Counties, etc., in northern Zhejiang, as well as Wujiang and Yixing in Jiangsu. The development of Huzhou opera roughly experienced three periods, namely little opera period, Huzhou Tanhuang drama period and script drama period.

船拳 Boat Boxing

船拳因在船上打拳而得名，发源于古吴兴地区即现在的练市、双林一带，古称"水战"。其套路丰富多彩，步法稳扎，躲闪灵活。

Boat boxing got its name because people practiced boxing on a boat. Originated in the ancient Wuxing area, which are now Lianshi and Shuanglin in Zhejiang Province, boat boxing was called "water battle" in ancient times. It has rich varieties of skills and tricks, featuring steady footwork and flexible dodge, etc.

文化寻踪之出行贴士 Travel Tips

寻踪之旅载体：南浔区双林镇菱文化节

寻踪之旅地点：浙江省湖州市南浔区双林镇

寻踪之旅时间：通常为9月中下旬

寻踪信息查询：(1)http://www.nanxun.gov.cn；(2)"南浔旅游"微信公众平台；(3)搜狐、腾讯等多家网站。

Cultural Activity: Water Caltrop Cultural Festival in Shuanglin

Town, Nanxun District

Ancient Town: Shuanglin Town, Nanxun District, Huzhou City, Zhejiang Province

Travel Time: Usually in mid to late September

For More Information: (1) Please visit http://www.nanxun.gov.cn; (2) Please search on the WeChat public platform "Nanxun Lvyou"; (3) Please visit the websites such as Sohu, Tencent, etc.

参考资料

http://www.bytravel.cn/Landscape/92/huanguqiaoqun.html

http://www.zjich.cn/xiangmu/xiangmushow.html?id=351

http://www.zjich.cn/xiangmu/xiangmushow.html?id=388

http://www.zjich.cn/xiangmu/xiangmushow.html?id=1006

https://mp.weixin.qq.com/s/YKz6fZhha2pN0D-Z5C1NMg

http://huznxsl.zjzwfw.gov.cn/index.html

https://timgsa.baidu.com/timg?image&quality=80&size=b9999_10000&sec=1608551155450&di=7b38c122f6f1c234d8a0a468d2eebc71&imgtype=0&src=http%3A%2F%2Fstc.zjol.com.cn%2Fg1%2FM00077DCggSDlar-Jt-ANM-uAAEaMXjZa58293.jpg%3Fwidth%3D500%26height%3D350

https://ss1.bdstatic.com/70cFvXSh_Q1YnxGkpoWK1HF6hhy/it/u=116600255,9189254&fm=26&gp=0.jpg

https://timgsa.baidu.com/timg?image&quality=80&size=b9999_10000&sec=1608551742399&di=8e25a9e8130da0117ba5d68506ae8b72&imgtype=0&src=http%3A%2F%2Fstc-new.8531.cn%2Fassets%2F20190731%2F1564574540806_5d41834c159bb86b9909326b.jpeg

https://timgsa.baidu.com/timg?image&quality=80&size=b9999_10000&sec=1608551886713&di=47cb70aec4a7648bd894a8c40b9c5657&imgtype=

0&src=http% 3A% 2F% 2F5b0988e595225. cdn. sohucs. com% 2Fimages% 2F20181217%2F97d4fdd74bec41aab6375a9198a4d3b8.jpeg

https://timgsa.baidu.com/timg?image&quality=80&size=b9999_10000&sec=1608552041261&di=c588fc6b97f65ecb62e335897300c041&imgtype=0&src=http%3A%2F%2Fphotocdn.sohu.com%2F20130510%2FImg375504113.jpg

http://regional.chinadaily.com.cn/huzhou/2020-03/10/c_408414.htm

https://www.sohu.com/a/120061129_448308

http://regional.chinadaily.com.cn/huzhou/2020-06/29/c_407935.htm

https://travel.qunar.com/p-oi10011463-shuanglinguzhen

https://www.sohu.com/a/273641288_383592

文化活动五：庆元菇神庙会

Cultural Activity (5): Mushroom God Temple Fair in Qingyuan

文化寻踪之浙里村落 Ancient Villages

➢ 庆元县松源镇大济村

Daji Village, Songyuan Town, Qingyuan County

大济村位于丽水庆元县城的南面，距县城2—3公里，村东南部群山环抱，西部河谷盆地，有济川溪从村中经过。大济村是一个古文化的聚集地，该村历代尊师重教，崇文尚礼，人才辈出。这个历史上不足300人的小村，自宋代至明代陆续涌现出26名进士。大济村还完整地保留着明清古居、木屋廊桥、金甃街、古井、古地道等诸多古迹文物。

Daji Village is located in the south of Qingyuan County, Lishui, which is two to three kilometers away from the county. The southeast part of the village is surrounded by mountains, and the western river valley is surrounded by the Jichuan River passing through the village. Daji Village is a gathering place of ancient culture. Generations of the village have respected teachers and education, valued culture and courtesy, therefore, talented people have emerged endlessly. This small village with less than 300 people in history had seen 26 presented scholars from the Song Dynasty to the Ming Dynasty. It also fully preserves many historical and cultural relics such as Ming and Qing ancient dwellings, wooden ceilinged bridges, Jinzhou Street, ancient wells, ancient tunnels.

文化寻踪之浙里印记 Cultural Imprints

➤ 建筑文化
Architectural Culture

明清古民居群 Ancient Dwellings in the Ming and Qing Dynasties

大济古村落以明清建筑为主，基本上为大济历史上名人的官宅，大部分厅堂还有皇帝或名人的题匾。明代民居的共同特点有：从大门进去不设倒座，多以三合院为整体布局，普遍选择坚硬木材制作形状不同的木柱础，造型古朴，采光良好。古民居建筑布局合理，墙高院深，工艺精细，威严壮观。设计师把防火、防风安全系数摆在首位，兼顾采光，通行实用为一体。现在的明清建筑有达德堂、聿新堂、树德堂、修德堂、慎修堂、世德堂、悒清楼等。

The ancient villages of Daji are dominated by Ming and Qing architectures, and are basically the official residences of celebrities in the history of Daji. Most halls have plaques inscribed by emperors or celebrities. Let's see the common features of Ming dwellings: there is no Daozuo (rooms facing north, usually for the servants to live) when entering from the gate, and the overall layout is the traditional quadrangle house. It is common to choose hard wood to make wooden pillar foundations of different shapes, which are simple in shape and good in lighting. The layout of the ancient residential buildings is reasonable, with high walls and deep courtyards, fine craftsmanship, and majestic grandeur. The designer put fire and wind safety factors in the first place, taking into account daylighting, traffic and practicality. The current Ming and Qing buildings include Dade Hall, Yuxin Hall, Shude Hall, Xiude Hall, Shenxiu Hall, Shide Hall, Yiqing Building, etc.

➢ 名人文化
Celebrity Culture

扁鹊卢医庙 The Temple of Doctor Lu (Bian Que)

扁鹊，战国初期齐国人，又号卢医。他是中医"望、闻、问、切"四诊方法的创始者，是一位杰出的医学家，留给后人的医学经典《难经》是中国医学的珍贵文献。人们一直怀念他，称其为"福神"。卢医庙又称卢福神庙、卢福庙、扁鹊庙等，始建于元惠宗至正元年(1341年)，为大济村先民纪念神医扁鹊而建。卢医庙建筑面积2300多平方米，是中国现存较为完整的古庙之一。其结构严谨、做工精细，既体现了宏伟的古代建筑风格，又融合了深厚的医学文化内涵与独特的地方民俗风情，具有重要的历史、艺术、科学价值。

Bian Que, a native of Qi in the early Warring States period, was also known as Doctor Lu. He is the founder of the Four Diagnostic Methods of TCM including "observation, listening, interrogation and pulse feeling", and is an outstanding physician. The medical classic *Classic on Medical Problems* left to future generations is a precious document of traditional Chinese medicine. The common people have always been missing him, calling him "the god of good fortune". The Temple of Doctor Lu, also known as the Temple of Good Fortune God, the Temple of Bian Que, etc., was built in the first year of emperor Huizong (1341) of the Yuan Dynasty to commemorate the genius doctor Bianque by the ancestors of Daji village. The Temple of Doctor Lu has a construction area of more than 2, 300 square meters and is one of the relatively complete ancient temples in existence in China. The rigorous structure and fine workmanship not only reflect the majestic architectural style, but also integrate the profound medical cultural connotation and unique local folk customs. It has an important historical, artistic and scientific value.

文化寻踪之出行贴士 Travel Tips

寻踪之旅载体:庆元菇神庙会

寻踪之旅地点:浙江省丽水市庆元县松源镇大济村

寻踪之旅时间:通常为9月

寻踪信息查询:(1)http://www.lishui.gov.cn;(2)"庆元旅游"微信公众平台;(3)搜狐、腾讯等多家网站。

Cultural Activity: Mushroom God Temple Fair in Qingyuan

Ancient Town: Daji Village, Songyuan Town, Qingyuan County, Lishui City, Zhejiang Province

Travel Time: Usually in September

For More Information: (1) Please visit http://www.lishui.gov.cn; (2) Please search on the WeChat public platform "Qingyuan Lvyou"; (3) Please visit the websites such as Sohu, Tencent, etc.

参考资料

https://baike.baidu.com/redirect/95adOjAwrpZa8erevpAxVldgf0hGUEUQwh08fvac5kKcIZij9ZZhz4on9014BmQks2Mr3Fzi548dP9lGTYTi55Jfzw9OB4PgwpHHkOye5o5kSA35iWWZnxCa1LK5AfDX7bwhHMRS1Ky5

https://baike. baidu. com/item/% E5%A4%A7%E6%B5%8E% E6%9D% 91/5742934

http://qynews.zjol.com.cn/qynews/system/2013/09/02/016878083.shtml

http://www.lishui.gov.cn/col/col1229216404/index.html

http://qynews.zjol.com.cn/qynews/system/2018/08/21/031089213.shtml

http://www.zjich.cn/xiangmu/xiangmushow.html?id=863

http://qynews.zjol.com.cn/qynews/system/2016/07/19/020607764.shtml

https://m.sohu.com/a/346413141_120054062/

文化活动六：赏桂花和红枫等特色树木

Cultural Activity (6):

Appreciating the Characteristic Trees Such as Osmanthus and Red Maples

文化寻踪之浙里村落 Ancient Villages

➢ 乐清市仙溪镇南阁村

Nange Village, Xianxi Town, Yueqing City

乐清市仙溪镇南阁村距今已有一千多年的历史，是明朝礼部尚书章纶的故里，坐落于雁荡山北麓，四周群山环抱，九曲溪自村北蜿蜒而过，风光旖旎，环境清幽，因与北阁村遥遥相对而得名。关于章氏遗迹，现存的有牌楼群、尚书第、笃忠堂以及墓葬等。2010年，南阁村获得了国家第五批“历史文化名村”的称号。

Nange Village, Xianxi Town, Yueqing City, has a history of more than a thousand years, and it is the hometown of Zhang Lun, the Minister of the Ministry of Rites of the Ming Dynasty. Located at the northern foot of Mountain Yandang, with mountains surrounded and the Jiuqu River winding through, the village boasts a beautiful scenery and tranquil environment, and it was named Nange ("nan" refers to the south) Village because of the opposite Beige ("bei" refers to the north) Village. Regarding Zhang Lun's relics, the archway group, his former residence, Duzhong Hall and the tomb are now well preserved. In 2010, Nange Village won the title of the fifth batch of national historical and cultural villages.

文化寻踪之浙里印记 Cultural Imprints

➢ 建筑文化
Architectural Culture

南阁牌楼群 The Memorial Archways of Nange Village

牌楼群是南阁的精髓，建于明正统四年（1439），原有7座，现存5座，分别为："世进士""恩光""方伯""尚书""会魁"。牌楼沿南阁村主街道从北至南依次纵向排列，全长150米，井然有序，气势不凡，是江南地区保存最完整、年代最早、数量最多的木构牌楼群。牌楼形制、结构相近，细部不同，具有明显的浙南地方建筑风格。

The memorial archways are the culture essence of Nange Village. Built in the fourth year of Emperor Zhengtong (1439) of the Ming Dynasty, five out of seven original archways are well preserved in the village, entitled respectively with "Shijinshi", "Enguang", "Fangbo", "Shangshu", and "Huikui". The archways are displayed vertically along the main street of Nange Village from north to south, with a total length of 150 meters, orderly and magnificently. The memorial archway group is regarded as the earliest, the largest and the most well preserved wooden archway group in the south of the Yangtze River, featuring the typical architectural style of south Zhejiang Province. The archway group not only reflects the local architectural culture and architectural style of the Ming Dynasty, but also showcases the outstanding achievements of Zhang Lun and his descendants.

名人文化
Celebrity Culture

章纶故居 The Former Residence of Zhang Lun

章纶，明代名臣、藏书家，以诗书自娱。章纶故居是章纶安享晚年之处，位于仙溪镇南阁村凤凰山脚下，坐南朝北，由照壁、台门、楼房、左右厢房组成，是宝贵的历史文化资源。故居原为三进合院式建筑，现存前后二进和笃忠堂，由藏书楼连接。笃忠堂现存一间，是章纶的儿子章玄应为祭祀章纶而建。藏书楼仅留原拱门的残垣断壁，内台门青砖平砌，中悬"尚书第"匾，基本保存了明代的风格。

Zhang Lun was a famous official and bibliophile in the Ming Dynasty. He amused himself with books or poems. The former residence of Zhang Lun was the place where Zhang Lun enjoyed his old age. It is located at the foot of Mountain Fenghuang in Nange Village, Xianxi Town, facing north, and is composed of a screen wall facing the gate of a house, Taimen, buildings and wing rooms, known as a precious non-renewable historical and cultural resource. The former residence was originally a three-row courtyard-style building, but now there are two rows of constructions left as well as Duzhong Hall, which are connected by the ancient library. Duzhong Hall has only one room now, which was built to worship Zhang Lun by his son Zhang Xuanying, and what is left in the library are the ruins of the original arches. Taimen was built with blue bricks and the plaque with the characters "Shang Shu Di" (meaning the minister's residence) is hung in the middle of the gate, which basically preserves the architectural style of the Ming Dynasty.

文化寻踪之出行贴士 Travel Tips

寻踪之旅载体:赏桂花和红枫等特色树木

寻踪之旅地点:浙江省温州市乐清市仙溪镇南阁村

寻踪之旅时间:通常为9月

寻踪信息查询:(1)http://www.yueqing.gov.cn/;(2)"诗画浙江文旅资讯"微信公众平台;(3)搜狐、腾讯等多家网站。

Cultural Activity: Appreciating the Characteristic Trees such as Osmanthus and Red Maples

Ancient Town: Nange Village, Xianxi Town, Yueqing City, Zhejiang Province

Travel Time: Usually in September

For More Information: (1) Please visit http://www.yueqing.gov.cn/; (2) Please search on the WeChat public platform "Shihua Zhejiang Wenlv Zixun"; (3) Please visit the websites such as Sohu, Tencent, etc.

参考资料

http://news.66wz.com/system/2013/08/05/103755768.shtml

http://www.yqcn.com/system/2014/04/03/011626576.shtml

http://www.wzxc.gov.cn/system/2013/08/16/011359136.shtml

http://www.tcmap.com.cn/zhejiangsheng/leqingshi_xianxizhen.html

http://news.66wz.com/system/2012/09/20/103366876.shtml

http://zhang1.zupu.cn/wenhua/352720.jhtml

http://www.tourunion.com/info/htm17/142772.htm

http://zjyq.wenming.cn/wztt/201512/t20151204_2172625.htm

http://www.yueqing.gov.cn/art/2018/11/6/art_1495324_23295797.html

http://www.yueqing.gov.cn/art/2019/10/17/art_1322072_38931841.html

http://www.yueqing.gov.cn/art/2019/8/7/art_1495324_36446407.html

http://wl.wenzhou.gov.cn/art/2019/10/30/art_1660367_39573670.html

http://tianqi.moji.com/liveview/picture/80684804

http://touch.travel.qunar.com/bookElement/6917510/2634593-2

http://www.theping.cn/e/action/ShowInfo.php?classid=173&id=34688

http://www.wzrb.com.cn/article503085show.html

10月 October

文化寻踪之推荐日历 Recommended Month

文化活动一：马仙出巡
Cultural Activity (1): Goddess Ma on Patrol

文化活动二：民俗文化节
Cultural Activity (2): Folk Culture Festival

文化活动三：红色文化教育（一）
Cultural Activity (3): Red Culture Education I

文化活动四：红色文化教育（二）
Cultural Activity (4): Red Culture Education II

文化活动五：红色文化教育（三）
Cultural Activity (5): Red Culture Education III

文化活动一：马仙出巡

Cultural Activity (1): Goddess Ma on Patrol

文化寻踪之浙里村落 Ancient Towns

➢ 平阳县顺溪镇

Shunxi Town, Pingyang County

顺溪镇位于浙江省温州市平阳县，拥有丰富独特的旅游资源。顺溪景区是国家级风景区——南雁荡山五大景区之一，素有“峰险、洞奇、岩怪、水美”之称。人文景观有顺溪古民居群以及百僧堂、陈氏宗祠、老街等景点，其中顺溪古民居群在2006年被列入国家级文物保护单位。顺溪镇保留了大量清代乾隆嘉庆年间建筑的民居，尤以陈氏宗族大屋保存最为完整。

Located in Pingyang County, Wenzhou City, Zhejiang Province, Shunxi Town boasts rich and unique tourism resources. Shunxi scenic spot is one of the five scenic spots of the South Yandang Mountain, the national-level scenic area, known for "the dangerous peaks, mysterious caves, rugged rocks and tranquil waters". The cultural landscape includes the ancient residential buildings in Shunxi, Baiseng Hall, Chen's Ancestral Hall, the old street and so on, among which the ancient residential buildings in Shunxi were listed as the historical and cultural site protected at the national level in 2006. Due to its rural location, Shunxi Town retains a large number of houses built during the reign of Emperor Qianlong and Emperor Jiaqing in the Qing Dynasty, of which the Chen clan houses were best preserved.

文化寻踪之浙里印记 Cultural Imprints

➢ 建筑文化
Architectural Culture

顺溪陈氏古民居群 Chen's Ancient Residential Buildings in Shunxi

顺溪陈氏民居，位于平阳县南雁荡山附近的顺溪镇。陈氏民居多为古建筑，始迁祖名陈育球，明隆庆间全家从温州市永嘉县大岙迁至顺溪。经过一百多年的繁育，传至清初陈嘉询一代，开始建造第一座大屋。陈氏民居样式与祖屋相似，只有面积大小有区别，现存大屋共五座：康乾年间陈嘉询祖屋，乾嘉间年陈显仁、陈安仁、陈作仁大屋，以及嘉道年间陈崇仁大屋。

Chen's residential buildings are located in Shunxi Town near the South Yandang Mountain in Pingyang County, most of which are ancient buildings.

During the Longqing period of the Ming Dynasty, their ancestor Chen Yuqiu moved with the whole family from Da'ao, Yongjia County to Shunxi, Wenzhou City. After more than 100 years, i.e. in the early Qing Dynasty, Chen Jiaxun began to build the first big house. The style of Chen's residential buildings is similar to those of the first ancestral houses, while the difference lies only in the size of the houses. There are five existing big houses, including Chen Jiaxun's (during the reign of Emperor Kangxi and Emperor Qianlong), Chen Xianren's, Chen Anren's, Chen Zuoren's (during the reign of Emperor Qianlong and Emperor Jiaqing) and Chen Chongren's (during the reign of Emperor Jiaqing and Emperor Daoguang) ancestral houses.

百僧堂 Baiseng Hall

百僧堂，正名云祥寺，背靠铁障峰。寺分旧寺和新寺两座，二者相距50米，建筑面积共800平方米。旧寺创建于元代至正七年(1347)，清康熙时重建，光绪七年(1881)再建，有7间平房。寺内保存摹像题记碑刻多块，其中有清宣统年间所镌之青石碑记一块，记述了该寺之兴衰历程。百僧堂既是著名的佛教场所，又拥有奇特的地貌与风景。

Baiseng Hall, with the official name Yunxiang Temple, is backed by the Tiezhang Peak. The temple is divided into two temples, the old one and the new one, 50 meters apart, with a total construction area of 800 square meters. The old temple was founded in the the seventh year of Zhizheng (1347) in the Yuan Dynasty, and rebuilt respectively in the reign of Emperor Kangxi of the Qing Dynasty, and in the seventh year of Emperor Guangxu (1881), with seven bungalows. There are many well preserved steles in the temple, engraved with epigraphs or drawings, among which there is a bluestone stele dates back to the Xuantong period of the Qing Dynasty, describing the history of the temple's rise and fall. Baiseng Hall is not only a famous Buddhist place, but also a scenic spot, where people could enjoy peculiar landforms and enchanting views.

➢ 非遗文化 Intangible Cultural Heritage

平阳木偶戏 Pingyang Puppet Show

平阳木偶戏包括提线、布袋、杖头、人偶四种类型，既可以单独表演，又可以综合演出。平阳木偶艺人最早创作了四种木偶类型，融为一体同台演出，这在全国都是个典型的例子。清末民初，平阳民间竟有一百多个木偶戏班社。中华人民共和国成立初期，政府创建了平阳县木偶剧团，具有里程碑意义。

Pingyang puppet show includes the following four types: marionette, glove puppet, rod puppet and the puppet show acted by real people, which can be performed individually or in group. Pingyang puppet artists first created the show that combined four types of puppets, which was regarded a typical example in the whole country. At the end of the Qing Dynasty and the beginning of the Republic of China, there were more than 100 puppet troupes in Pingyang. In the early days of the founding of the People's Republic of China, the government established Pingyang Puppet Troupe.

马仙信俗 Goddess Ma Belief and Custom

马仙信俗，是景宁畲族自治县最具影响力的女神信仰，是将马仙信仰和民间道教科仪及民俗活动相结合的仪式活动，时间在每年的七月初至

七月中旬。仪式前三天，全城禁止屠杀，戒荤沐浴，洒扫街头、通道、门庭，清洗泉井、溪流。仪式主要由“迎神”“献祭”“巡境”“醮仪”“送神”等五个部分组成，每一个部分都有其独特丰富的传统文化内涵。这一习俗已存在五百多年，是民间传统信仰习俗的遗存现象。

Goddess Ma belief and custom is the most influential goddess belief in Jingning She Autonomous County. It is a ritual activity combining Goddess Ma belief with folk Taoist ritual and folk activities, which is held from early July to mid-July in the lunar calendar every year. Three days before the ceremony, slaughtering is forbidden and bathing is required in the whole city, streets, passageways and courtyards are swept, and springs, wells and streams are cleaned. The ceremony is mainly composed of five parts, including welcoming the goddess, offering sacrifices, patrolling, paying tributes to the goddess, and seeing off the goddess. Each part has its unique and rich traditional cultural connotation. This custom has existed for more than 500 years and is a relic of traditional folk belief and custom.

平阳太平钿剪纸 Pingyang Taipingdian Paper Cutting

平阳太平钿剪纸与民俗有着密切的联系，旧时凡逢年过节等喜庆活动，常用相应的太平钿剪纸装扮屋内的门窗和墙壁，并摆放在各式瓜果点心上，点缀喜庆和吉祥。平阳太平钿剪纸历史悠久，其用小纸片拧成针状，作为“订书针”

来装订红纸，该装订方法沿用至今，为“剪纸艺术是历史的活化石”一说提供了佐证。“平阳太平钿剪纸”这一名称体现了民众祈求太平的愿望。剪纸外观呈方形或圆形，处在字样当中的大多为铜钱或花环形图案，字样按上下右左中排列。

Pingyang Taipingdian paper cutting has a close relationship with folk custom. In the old days, the corresponding Taipingdian paper cutting works were often used to decorate the doors, windows and walls of the house, and put on fruits and snacks to decorate the festive and auspicious activities. Pingyang Taipingdian paper cutting has a long history. Small pieces of paper were twisted into needles and used as “staples” to bind red paper. This binding method has been used from then to today, which provides evidence for the theory that “paper cutting art is a living fossil of history”. The name of Pingyang Taipingdian paper cutting reflects the people’s desire for peace. The appearance of the paper cutting is square or round. In the middle of most paper cutting words are copper coin or flower ring patterns. The words are arranged on the top, bottom, right, left and middle.

平阳吹打 Pingyang Wind and Percussion Instruments Playing

吹打，是昆曲曲段连串起来并配以丝竹和打击乐器进行吹拉弹唱的一种民间乐曲。它起源于平阳，流行于温州市区、泰顺等地。演戏前常要打头通，俗称“闹场”。头通一敲，观众便从四面八方赶来。以笛子为主奏，配以板胡、二胡、三弦等弹拨乐器，以及鼓板、梆子、牛皮鼓等打击乐器，民间称之为“集锦”。

This kind of playing is a kind of folk music in which Kunqu opera segments are linked together and accompanied by wind and percussion instruments. It originated in Pingyang, and became popular in Wenzhou, Taishun and other areas. In the past, such music was necessary, i. e. warming up music should be played before the show. The audience came from all places as soon as they heard the music. It is mainly played by Chinese flute, accompanied by Banhu, Erhu, Sanxian and other plucked instruments, as well as percussion instruments such as Guban, Bangzi and cowhide drum. The mixture of instruments are called "Jijin" (a collection) by the locals.

文化寻踪之出行贴士 Travel Tips

寻踪之旅载体:马仙出巡

寻踪之旅地点:浙江省温州市平阳县顺溪镇

寻踪之旅时间:通常为10月中旬

寻踪信息查询:(1)http://www.zjpy.gov.cn;(2)"平阳旅游"微信公众平台;(3)搜狐、腾讯等多家网站。

Cultural Activity: Goddess Ma on Patrol

Ancient Town: Shunxi Town, Pingyang County, Zhejiang Province

Travel Time: Usually in mid-October

For More Information: (1) Please visit http://www.zjpy.gov.cn; (2) Please search on the WeChat public platform "Pingyang Lvyou"; (3) Please visit the websites such as Sohu, Tencent, etc.

参考资料

https://baike.sogou.com/v64610636.htm?fromTitle=顺溪镇

https://baike.sogou.com/v74487879.htm?fromTitle=顺溪陈氏民居
https://mp.weixin.qq.com/s/cVFwtvRV9pMDax5cNDxEXA
http://www.zjich.cn/xiangmu/xiangmushow.html?id=372
http://www.zjich.cn/xiangmu/xiangmushow.html?id=2336
http://www.zjich.cn/xiangmu/xiangmushow.html?id=747
http://www.zjich.cn/xiangmu/xiangmushow.html?id=621
https://gimg2. baidu. com/image_search/src=http% 3A% 2F% 2Fwww. cphoto. com.cn%2Fdz%2Fattachments%2Fmonth_1510%2F15101606164a82842706bdc5e9.jpg&refer=http%3A%2F%2Fwww.cphoto.com.cn&app=2002&size=f9999,10000&q=a80&n=0&g=0n&fmt=jpeg?sec=1612531789&t=d4c5fb669cc49ba5abf06f957dfd2f74
https://gimg2. baidu. com/image_search/src=http% 3A% 2F% 2Fimg. mp. itc. cn%2Fupload%2F20161110%2Fc4960114de4b4a38aee78ef0f96b9482_th. jpeg&refer=http% 3A% 2F% 2Fimg. mp. itc. cn&app=2002&size=f9999,10000&q=a80&n=0&g=0n&fmt=jpeg?sec=1612531968&t=d4585da0d115874d7f382cdc174d0b82
https://gimg2. baidu. com/image_search/src=http% 3A% 2F% 2Fimg1001. pocoimg.cn%2Fimage%2Fpoco%2Fworks%2F40%2F2011%2F1104%2F22%2F55441840201111042256408436227143995_002_55441840.jpg&refer=http% 3A% 2F% 2Fimg1001. pocoimg. cn&app=2002&size=f9999,10000&q=a80&n=0&g=0n&fmt=jpeg?sec=1612532074&t=e8164c17ca1b91ef1c8c055985e02cf4
https://ss3.bdstatic.com/70cFv8Sh_Q1YnxGkpoWK1HF6hhy/it/u=3153346601,842449072&fm=26&gp=0.jpg
https://gimg2. baidu. com/image_search/src=http% 3A% 2F% 2Fimg. pconline. com.cn%2Fimages%2Fupload%2Fupc%2Ftx%2Fphotoblog%2F1008%2F23%2Fc5%2F4954443_4954443_1282574908703. jpg&refer=http% 3A% 2F% 2Fimg. pconline. com. cn&app=2002&size=f9999, 10000&q=a80&n=0&g=0n&fmt=jpeg?sec=1612532441&t=0b4a8ff67b74fb5b928faa1569f51121

https://ss1.bdstatic.com/70cFvXSh_Q1YnxGkpoWK1HF6hhy/it/u=98473935, 3362100874&fm=15&gp=0.jpg

http://sjk.zjich.cn/ImageData/loadImageData.page?ViewSize=large&DataOwner=XM_ML_DANGAN_FENGMIAN&DataID=227813

http://sjk.zjich.cn/ImageData/loadImageData.page?ViewSize=large&DataOwner=XM_ML_DANGAN_FENGMIAN&DataID=227847

https://www.sohu.com/a/293395860_355926

http://www.zjpy.gov.cn/art/2016/11/21/art_1250922_3322424.html

https://www.travelchinaguide.com/intro/arts/paper_cut.htm

文化活动二：民俗文化节

Cultural Activity (2): Folk Culture Festival

文化寻踪之浙里村落 Ancient Villages

➢ 金华市前仓镇厚吴村

Houwu Village, Qiancang Town, Jinhua City

厚吴村位于浙江省金华市前仓镇，面积2.45平方公里。厚吴村现存永康农村第一大古建筑群，村内存有宋、元、明、清朝代的厅堂楼宇、民宅大院、庐墅精舍近百幢，总数1000多间。厚吴村还拥有永康市最早创办的小学和创办已逾百年、历史最悠久的村级婺剧团。这个有着近800年历史的吴氏聚居村落基本保存了原有的格局，巷道纵横，池塘密集，水系清晰，古建筑连绵成片，类型齐全，涵盖公共建筑、商业建筑、宗祠建筑和住宅建筑等，极具历史价值。

Houwu Village is located in Qiancang Town, Jinhua City, Zhejiang

Province, covering an area of 2.45 square kilometers. Houwu Village has the largest ancient architectural complex in Yongkang rural area. There are nearly 100 halls, houses, courtyards, and villas of the Song, Yuan, Ming and Qing Dynasties, totaling more than 1,000 rooms. Houwu Village also boasts the earliest primary school of Yongkang City and the oldest village-level Wu Opera Troupe that has been founded for more than 100 years. This residential village of Wu family with a history of almost 800 years has basically preserved the original pattern, with vertical and horizontal roadways, dense ponds, and clear water system. The ancient architectural complex is of great historical value, and covers various types including buildings of public, commercial, ancestral and residential uses.

文化寻踪之浙里印记 Cultural Imprints

➢ 建筑文化
Architectural Culture

吴氏宗祠 Wu's Ancestral Hall

吴氏宗祠始建于明嘉靖二十六年(1547),占地1140多平方米,现除花砖门楼是初建遗构外,其余建筑都是清光绪年间重建的。该宗祠前后三进,规模宏大。正对水池前的空地原有六座巍峨的青石牌坊,目前仅有一些残件还散落在祠堂内。门厅三间,外有抱鼓石、旗杆礅等,左右五花山墙上有墨书“文谟”“武烈”和一些水墨画,正中大门石刻“吴氏宗祠”。中厅“叙伦堂”五间,石柱木梁,九架抬梁结构,粗大的额枋上悬挂着数十块匾额和一方家规,大多是明清原物,稍间山墙砖壁的“忠孝廉节”四个翰墨大字也是难得的书法精品。后寝七间，五明二暗，供奉着吴氏世代先辈的牌位。两侧厢房二十余间，同样挂满古匾。

Wu's Ancestral Hall was built in the 26th year (1547) of Jiajing in the Ming Dynasty, covering an area of more than 1,140 square meters. Now, apart from the brick gatehouse that was a relic of the initial constructions, the rest were rebuilt during the Guangxu period of the Qing Dynasty. The ancestral hall has three rows of constructions and is very large in scale. The front of the pool once stood six majestic bluestone memorial archways, while now only the fragments scatter in the hall. The front hall has three rooms. Outside the hall, there are drum-shaped stones, flagpole stones, etc. There are calligraphic works "Wen Mo" (文谟), "Wu Lie" (武烈) and some ink paintings on the left and right walls, and the Chinese characters "Wu's Ancestral Hall" (吴氏宗祠) are engraved on a big gate stone. The middle hall has five rooms. These rooms built with stone columns, wooden beams and the nine structure lifting girders. Dozens of plaques and domestic discipline and family rules have been hung on the large architrave, most of which are originals of the Ming and Qing Dynasties. The four Chinese characters of "Zhong, Xiao, Lian, Jie" ("Loyalty, Filial Piety, Honesty and Integrity") on the gable and brick walls are also rare calligraphy works. The back sleeping area has seven bedrooms, among which five are rooms with front view and two with rear view, enshrined with memorial tablets of the ancestors of Wu family. More than twenty wing rooms on both sides are decorated with ancient plaques.

➢ 非遗文化
Intangible Cultural Heritage

永康“打罗汉”Yongkang “Human Pyramid”

永康“打罗汉”是方岩庙会的主要内容之一，时间为八月初到九月中旬。相传，北宋时的兵部侍郎——胡则(浙江永康人)，倡导“蓄兵于民”，

主张闲时把农民集中起来，组织团练，练武强身，以便抵抗外敌入侵。在任时，他清正廉明，颇有政绩，百姓感恩之，遂于方岩山顶（胡则少时念书之地）建庙以纪念。永康的后人，便以村为单位进行自编的“打罗汉”活动演出，用“打罗汉”形式纪念胡则的生日。到了明代，戚继光任台（州）金（华）参将时，在金华募兵利用“打罗汉”练武，队伍骁勇善战，抗倭屡立奇功，“打罗汉”遂在金华的多个县市的民间流传开来。活动分为三个部分：第一段，走阵；第二段，民间武术表演；第三段，叠罗汉与民间艺术表演。永康叠罗汉以头旗为主导，以锣鼓班和乐队助演。压轴戏是叠罗汉，形式有竖牌坊、彩塔叠、叠香亭、荷花翻叶、游城、拜观音、十八洞、过仙桥等，至今有近千年的历史。

The performance of Yongkang “Human Pyramid” is one of the main content of Fangyan Temple Fair, which is held from lunar August 1st to mid-September. According to legend, when Hu Ze (a native of Yongkang, Zhejiang) was the vice minister of the Ministry of War, he advocated that all of the unemployed farmers should gather together and practice Kungfu so as to resist foreign invasion. Yongkangers' descendants bear the custom in mind, so they took village as a unit and continued to hold the self-compiled performance “Human Pyramid”. The activity is particularly bustling on Hu Ze's birthday. In the Ming Dynasty, Qi Jiguang served as a general in Taizhou and Jinhua. He recruited soldiers in Jinhua and trained them in the form of human pyramid. The soliders he trained were brave and skillful in fighting against the Japanese pirates, therefore, the custom of Human Pyramid had been spread among the people in many counties and cities of Jinhua. The activity is divided into three parts: the first part is the walking formation; the second part is the folk martial arts performance; the third part is the Human Pyramid and folk art performance. Yongkang “Human Pyramid” is dominated by the head flag and assisted by gongs, drums and bands. The finale is the performance of human pyramid which has s a history of nearly a thousand years, with forms such as vertical archway, color pagoda stacking, stacking incense pavilion, lotus leaf turning, city tour, worshiping Avalokitesvara, eighteen holes, crossing fairy bridge, etc.

婺剧 Wu Opera

婺剧俗称金华戏,是我国古老的剧种之一,流传区域广。婺剧源于明朝中叶。它原汁原味地保留了高腔、昆曲、乱弹、徽调、滩簧、时调等多种声腔,其表演还保留着秦汉以来各种艺术表演的痕迹。脚本文辞典雅,叙事通俗易懂。在表演过程中,有自己独特的行头和化装形态,特别善于文戏武做、武戏文做,堪称一绝。婺剧剧目丰富,有500多种,以口传为主,传统深厚,特色浓郁,影响深广,有“徽戏活化石”之称,是我国戏剧表演艺术的瑰宝。

Wu opera, commonly known as Jinhua opera, is one of the ancient operas and spreads widely in China. Originated in the middle of the Ming Dynasty, Wu opera has originally preserved a variety of tune patterns, such as high-pitched tune, Kun opera tune, Luantan tune, Anhui opera tune, Tanhuang tune and Shi tune, etc., and its performances also retain the traces of various artistic performances since the Qin and Han Dynasties. The scripts of Wu opera are elegant and the narrative is easy to understand. Wu opera has its own unique costumes and makeup for performance, and it is particularly good at performing martial arts. It has a rich repertoire of more than 500 programs, most of which passed down in the form of oral transmission, with profound traditions, strong characteristics, and profound influence. It is mainly preformed in oral, with profound traditions, distinct characteristics, and far-reaching influence. Therefore, it is reputed as the "living fossil" of Anhui opera and a treasure of our country's drama performance.

文化寻踪之出行贴士 Travel Tips

寻踪之旅载体:民俗文化节

寻踪之旅地点:浙江省金华市前仓镇厚吴村

寻踪之旅时间:通常为10月

寻踪信息查询:(1)http://jinhua.zjol.com.cn;(2)"金华非遗"微信公众平台;(3)搜狐、腾讯等多家网站。

Cultural Activity: Folk Culture Festival

Ancient Town: Houwu Village, Qiancang Town, Jinhua City, Zhejiang Province

Travel Time: Usually in October

For More Information: (1) Please visit http://jinhua. zjol. com. cn; (2) Please search on the WeChat public platform "Jinhua Feiyi"; (3) Please visit the websites such as Sohu, Tencent, etc.

参考资料

http://www.360doc.com/content/15/0411/13/11005683_462389992.shtml

https://www.douban.com/note/725622303/

https://baike. baidu. com/item/% E5%8E% 9A% E5%90%B4%E6%9D% 91/9618174?fr=aladdin

https://www.meipian.cn/2ilnp3d4

http://www.zjich.cn/xiangmu/xiangmushow.html?id=1018

https://www.meipian.cn/2lbw4k6s
https://weibo. com/p/1001603751425053163823? luicode=10000011&lfid=1076032036563431
http://www.zjich.cn/xiangmu/xiangmulist.html?keyword=%u5A7A%u5267
http://www.xi-qu.com/wj/ls/8186.html
http://www.xi-qu.com/wj/zs/
http://www.xi-qu.com/wj/zs/11577.html
http://www.xi-qu.com/wj/ts/8187.html
https://tieba.baidu.com/f?kw=%E5%A9%BA%E5%89%A7&ie=utf-8&tab=good
http://www.360doc.com/content/20/0305/12/1202041_896862501.shtml
https://v.zjol.com.cn/video/321391.html
https://www.xcar.com.cn/bbs/viewthread.php?tid=95945763
http://en.chinaculture.org/classics/2013-09/06/content_482002.htm

文化活动三:红色文化教育(一)

Cultural Activity (3):

Red Culture Education I

文化寻踪之浙里村落 Ancient Villages

➢ 永嘉县岩坦镇屿北村

Yubei Village, Yantan Town, Yongjia County

永嘉县岩坦镇屿北村生态平衡,环境清幽,村庄格局别具风貌,文物古迹比比皆是。环村有9座寨门、2道寨墙、1条护寨河和7座大小桥梁。村内过去有7座宗祠,其中以始建于南宋淳熙十三年(1186)的尚书祠最为著名。此外,村内还有30多座古宅和40余座四合院大屋,每座院子都有一个典雅的"堂"名,每个"堂"又都是一个与百姓生活息息相关的作坊。整个村落犹如陶渊明笔下的世外桃源。屿北是我党抗日战争中后期永嘉县开展游击战争的指挥中心,也是浙南地区重要的革命根据地。

Yubei Village, Yantan Town, Yongjia County has an ecological balance, a tranquil environment, a unique village layout, with abound cultural relics and historic sites. There are nine gates, two walls, a river, and seven bridges around the village. There used to be seven ancestral halls in the village, among which the most famous building was Minister's Ancestral Hall. These halls were built in the thirteenth year of Chunxi (1186) in the Southern Song Dynasty. In addition, there are more than 30 ancient houses and more than 40 quadrangles, each courtyard having an elegant name, which is a workshop closely related to the life of the people. The whole village is like a paradise described by Tao Yuanming, a famous poet in China. Yubei was also the command center for guerrilla warfare carried out in Yongjia County in the middle and late stages of the Anti-Japanese War of Chinese Communist Party, and an important revolutionary base in southern Zhejiang.

文化寻踪之浙里印记 Cultural Imprints

➢ 建筑文化 Architectural Culture

尚书祠 Minister's Ancestral Hall

尚书祠位于永嘉县岩坦镇屿北村，坐西朝东，系一座“曰”字形四合院式木构建筑，为纪念南宋“世尚书”汪应辰及子汪逵而建。始建于南宋淳熙三年(1176)，清乾隆五十三年(1788)重修，后又经多次修缮，占地面积3200平方米。尚书祠以轴线布局，由敕门、照壁、前厅、中厅、两厢轩、敦睦祠组成。其中，敦睦祠面阔五开间，设前檐廊，梁柱用材粗壮，明间20柱，次梢间各14柱，柱为四边形，梁架结构为抬梁与穿斗式结合。山墙用木板隔断，悬山顶屋面。明间正中悬挂乾隆五十年（1785）“敦睦”横匾。

Minister's Ancestral Hall is located in Yubei Village, Yantan Town, Yongjia County. Sitting in the west and facing east, it is a wooden quadrangle house with two rows of constructions. The hall was built to commemorate the two ministers in ancient China in the Southern Song Dynasty, Wang Yingchen and his son Wang Kui. The hall was firstly built in the third year of Chunxi (1176) in the Southern Song Dynasty. Then it was rebuilt in the fifty-third year of Emperor Qianlong (1788) of the Qing Dynasty, and later had been repaired many times. The ancestral hall covers an area around 3,200 square meters, and it is laid out on an axis. In addition, it consists of the imperial gate, the Zhaobi (a screen wall facing the gate of a house), the front hall, the middle hall, the wing rooms, and the Dunmu Ancestral Hall, etc. Among them, the Dunmu Ancestral Hall has five rooms wide, with front eaves and sturdy beams and pillars. There are 20 pillars in the main room and 14 pillars in other rooms, all of which are quadrilateral in shape. The gable is partitioned by wooden boards, and is in the design of overhanging gable roof. In the middle of the main room, a horizontal plaque "Dun Mu" is hung on the wall that could date back to the 50th year of Qianlong (1785).

➢ 非遗文化
Intangible Cultural Heritage

永嘉乱弹 Yongjia Luantan

永嘉乱弹也称“温州乱弹”，是浙江三大乱弹之一（另外两种是绍兴乱弹和金华乱弹），唱腔高昂粗朴，念白由温州方言和普通话杂糅而成，地域特色显著，1959年改称瓯剧。永嘉乱弹是温州地区最有影响的戏曲剧种，它大约形成于清代初年，主要在浙江温州各县及丽水、台州部分地区流传，影响远及闽北及赣东北一带。永嘉乱弹是一个多声腔剧种，以乱弹腔为主，兼唱昆腔、高腔、徽调、滩簧及时调等。剧目共有450余种，基本来自南戏、元明杂剧及明清传奇。

Yongjia luantan or Wenzhou luantan, later known as Ou opera since 1959, is a regional form of Chinese opera from Yongjia County, Wenzhou. In addition to Wenzhou and parts of neighboring Lishui and Taizhou (all in Zhejiang), it is also influential in parts of northern Fujian and northeastern Jiangxi. The earliest form of Yongjia luantan, however, developed in the beginning of the Qing Dynasty, when the singing styles of gaoqiang and kunqiang gained popularity in southern Zhejiang. The luantan style arrived later and was co-opted by locals in their performances along with gaoqiang and kunqiang. Because luantan proved the most popular vocal style, it dominated the form which gradually became known as Yongjia luantan or Wenzhou luantan. There are more than 450 kinds of repertoire, basically from southern opera, zaju plays in the Yuan and Ming Dynasties, and legends from the Ming and Qing Dynasties.

➤ 红色文化
Red Culture

中共瓯北中心县委旧址钟寿堂 Zhongshou Hall, the Site of the Central County Committee of the CCP in North Wenzhou

屿北村曾是土地革命战争时期红十三军活动的中心区域之一，村子东北角寨墙边上的一座古宅就是1943—1945年中共瓯北中心县委的驻地。1945年3月2日，国民党永嘉警备队30余

人偷袭屿北失败,而后国民党军队数次进犯屿北,均遭阻击。屿北武装起义在浙南瓯北地区革命斗争历史上具有重要的历史意义。为纪念屿北武装起义,1985年,在屿北村口建造了纪念碑亭,现为永嘉县爱国教育基地。

Yubei Village was one of the central areas of the 13th Red Army's activities during the Agrarian Revolutionary War. Zhongshou Hall, an ancient house on the edge of the wall in the northeast corner of the village, was the site of the Central County Committee of the Communist Party of China in north Wenzhou from 1943 to 1945. On March 2, 1945, more than 30 members of the Kuomintang's Yongjia garrison failed in a surprise attack on the north of the Yubei. Afterwards, the Kuomintang troops invaded the village several times and were blocked. The armed uprising in Yubei is a major event of great historical significance in the history of the revolutionary struggle in the northern Wenzhou region of southern Zhejiang. To commemorate the armed uprising in Yubei, a monument pavilion was built at the entrance of the village in 1985, and it is now a patriotic education base of Yongjia County.

文化寻踪之出行贴士 Travel Tips

寻踪之旅载体:红色文化教育(一)

寻踪之旅地点:浙江省温州市永嘉县岩坦镇屿北村

踪之旅时间:10月

寻踪信息查询:(1)http://www.yjnet.cn;(2)"永嘉文旅体资讯"微信公众平台;(3)搜狐、腾讯等多家网站。

Cultural Activity: Red Culture Education I

Ancient Village: Yubei Village, Yantan Town, Yongjia County, Wenzhou City, Zhejiang Province

Travel Time: October

For More Information: (1) Please visit http://www. yjnet. cn; (2) Please search on the WeChat public platform “Yongjia Wenlvti Zixun”; (3) Real-time information can be retrieved through Sohu, Tencent and other websites.

参考资料

https://zj.zjol.com.cn/red_boat.html?id=100675250

http://www.zjich.cn/news/newslist.html?keyword=%u6C38%u5609%u4E71%u5F39

http://www.zjich.cn/news/newsshow.html?id=442636

https://zj.zjol.com.cn/news/662199.html

http://www.zhongguogucunluo.com/zjgc/html/?32.html

http://www.360doc.com/content/15/0414/19/11005683_463205516.shtml

https://baijiahao.baidu.com/s?id=1641947746396257075&wfr=spider&for=pc

http://www.yjnet.cn/system/2018/07/27/013349223.shtml

http://yjltw.wzlib.cn/ltgk/ltqy/201306/t20130618_154040.htm

http://www.ihchina.cn/project_details/13487

http://www.sohu.com/a/273582089_720210

文化活动四：红色文化教育（二）

Cultural Activity (4): Red Culture Education II

文化寻踪之浙里村落 Ancient Towns

➢ 永嘉县岩头镇

Yantou Town, Yongjia County

岩头镇位于国家重点风景名胜区楠溪江的中游，是一个以山地为主、河谷盆地兼备的半山区乡镇，是温州市目前唯一的中国历史文化名镇，也是工农红军第十三军的诞生地，拥有独特的“古色、绿色、红色”旅游资源。岩头镇拥有“四张名片”：一是人口大镇，二是文化名镇，三是旅游城镇，四是战略重镇。全镇有晚唐以来的古村落和狮子岩景区等，其中“七星八斗”芙蓉村、“文房四宝”苍坡村、“金山丽水”岩头村别具一格，颇有盛名。

Located in the middle reach of the Nanxi River—the national key scenic spot, Yantou Town is surrounded by mountains and valleys, having both river valleys and basins. It is currently the only Chinese historical and cultural town in Wenzhou and the birthplace of the 13th Red Army, possessing the unique "tricolor" tourism resources, namely resources of "traditional colour, green colour and red colour". Yantou Town has "four name cards": a town with a large population, a famous historical and cultural town, a tourist town and a strategic town. The town has ancient villages built since the late Tang Dynasty, and Shiziyan Scenic Area, etc. Among them, Furong Village, Cangpo Village, and Yantou Village are the most unique and well-known representatives.

文化寻踪之浙里印记 Cultural Imprints

➢ 建筑文化 Architectural Culture

芙蓉村古建筑群 Ancient Complex in Furong Village

芙蓉村的建筑多为清代建造，包括民居、庙宇等建筑都保留了楠溪江古民居所固有的风貌古朴的特点。村中古建筑群由寨墙、寨门、民居、宗祠、牌坊、庙宇、书院、路亭等组成。村落呈东西窄、南北长的长方形布局，寨墙由不规则块石垒砌。芙蓉村古建筑的代表有陈氏大宗祠、三星祠、芙蓉书院、将军屋等。建筑出檐深远，大开间，短进深，大天井。建筑空间多院落组合，建筑小巧通透，朴实而又精致，质朴又带有灵气，有浙南民居的典型特征。

Most of the buildings in Furong Village were built in the Qing

Dynasty. The buildings, including residential buildings and temples, etc., have retained the inherent simplicity of the ancient residential buildings near the Nanxi River. The ancient complex in the village is composed of walls, gates, dwellings, ancestral halls, archways, temples, academies and pavilions, etc. The village has a rectangular layout, which is narrow from east to west and long from north to south, and the walls were built with irregular block stones. Representatives of the complex include Chen's Ancestral Hall, Sanxing Ancestral Hall, Furong Academy, the General's House, etc. With the deep eaves, large rooms, short row distances, large patio, the ancient dwellings feature multiple courtyards, and small-size, simple and exquisite design, which are the typical characteristics of southern Zhejiang residences.

金昭牌坊 Jin Zhao Memorial Archway

金昭,明朝进士。金昭牌坊为金昭进士及第时所建,俗称进士牌坊。金昭牌坊坐西朝东,面阔三间,为六柱三开间三楼式木构建筑,平面呈横长方形。牌楼两外侧立有四角柱。柱子用材粗壮,前后置抱鼓石。明间两柱为方石柱,次间两柱为木柱。明、次间屋脊还分别饰龙首吻、凤首吻,可谓是温州牌楼中的上乘之作。

Jin Zhao was a Jinshi (the presented scholar in the Ming Dynasty). Jin Zhao Memorial Archway was built when Jin Zhao passed the imperial examination and was titled Jinshi, therefore, it is commonly known as Jinshi Memorial Archway. Facing east, the archway has three rooms, and it is a three-floor wooden rectangular construction with six columns. There are four-corner columns on the two outer sides of the archway, which are made of sturdy materials, with well-designed drum stones on the front and the back. The two pillars in the middle are ashlar ones, and the two on its side are wooden ones. The roofs of the two are also decorated with the dragon and the phoenix, which can be regarded as the best of Wenzhou archways.

➢ 非遗文化
Intangible Cultural Heritage

永嘉花鼓 Yongjia Huagu (Flower Drum)

永嘉花鼓是一种古老的、独具地方特色的曲艺曲种。其以永嘉方言演唱，由一人一边演唱，一边用锣鼓伴奏，音乐简洁明快，唱腔动听，演唱内容包含了当地的文化、民俗、历史等各个领域。永嘉花鼓具有很强的地域特色，其在长期的演唱实践中吸收当地民歌精华，经不断融合形成了别具一格的演唱风格。

Yongjia Huagu is an ancient folk art with unique local characteristics. Singing in Yongjia dialect, one performer sings with gongs and drums accompanied. The music is concise and lively. The singing is pleasant. The content of the singing covers various fields, such as local culture, folk custom, and history. Yongjia Huagu performance has strong local features, since it has absorbed the essence of local folk songs in the long-term singing practice and has formed its own unique singing style after continous integration.

红色文化
Red Culture

红十三军旧址 The Former Site of the Military Headquarters of the 13th Red Army

红十三军军部旧址系四合院木构建筑，素有“永嘉的延安”之称。红十三军直属中央军委领导，是当时编入正式序列的全国十四支红军之一。旧址由纪念碑广场、军部旧址、红十三军历史纪念馆三部分组成，整体格局呈“口”字形。旧址正门上方横匾镌刻着张爱萍将军题写的“中国工农红军第十三军军部旧址”，是研究红十三军开展革命斗争历史的重要遗存。

The former site of the military headquarters of the 13th Red Army, is a quadrangle wooden structure, and is reputed as “Yongjia’s Yan’an”. The 13th Red Army was directly under the leadership of the Central Military Commission. It was one of 14 groups of the Red Army that was incorporated into the official sequence at that time. The site consists of three parts, namely the monument square, the former site of the military headquarters and the historical memorial hall of the 13th Red Army. The overall layout is in the shape of a Chinese character “口”. There is a plaque above the main entrance engraved with the epigraph by the General Zhang Aiping, which literally mean “the Former Site of the Military Headquarters of the 13th Red Army”. The site is an important relic of the history of the revolutionary struggle of the 13th Red Army.

文化寻踪之出行贴士 Travel Tips

寻踪之旅载体:红色文化教育(二)

寻踪之旅地点:浙江省温州市永嘉县岩头镇

寻踪之旅时间:10月

寻踪信息查询:(1)http://www.yj.gov.cn;(2)"温州古道"微信公众平台;(3)搜狐、腾讯等多家网站。

Cultural Activity: Red Culture Education II

Ancient Town: Yantou Town, Yongjia County, Wenzhou City, Zhejiang Province

Travel Time: October

For More Information: (1) Please visit http://www.yj.gov.cn; (2) Please search on the WeChat public platform "Wenzhou Gudao"; (3) Please visit the websites such as Sohu, Tencent, etc.

参考资料

https://town.zjol.com.cn/system/2016/11/01/021351700.shtml

http://www.tcmap.com.cn/zhejiangsheng/yongjiaxian_yantouzhen.html

http://epaper.wzrb.com.cn/content.aspx?id=335696

http://news.66wz.com/system/2017/08/23/105020069.shtml

https://town.zjol.com.cn/zxz/201806/t20180608_7500802.shtml

http://wl.wenzhou.gov.cn/art/2019/10/18/art_1660367_38963413.html

http://wzgmj.wzlib.cn/gmjyx/201608/t20160808_204326.htm

http://www.zhongguogucunluo.com/sts/html/?208.html

http://wenzhou.lvyou114.com/jingdian/jinshipailou/profile

http://wl.wenzhou.gov.cn/art/2015/9/22/art_1653048_34538415.html

http://wzgpf.db.wzlib.cn/detail.html?id=272&isTopic=0

https://new.qq.com/rain/a/20200423A0L7XX00

http://gov.66wz.com/system/2013/06/26/103701124.shtml

https://www.sohu.com/a/347658692_160274

https://mp.weixin.qq.com/s/fkVKDnHr0k5DXNDDCz07Sw

http://www.zjich.cn/news/newsshow.html?id=441569

https://baike.baidu.com/item/%E6%B0%B8%E5%98%89%E8%8A%B1%E9%BC%93/22842912?fr=aladdin

http://news.66wz.com/system/2015/05/15/104448370.shtml

http://wl.wenzhou.gov.cn/art/2015/9/22/art_1653048_34538414.html

http://www.yj.gov.cn/col/col1251788/index.html

http://www.wzdj.gov.cn/system/2009/12/29/101599043.shtml

http://edu.wenzhou.gov.cn/art/2018/10/18/art_1329835_21988046.html

https://www.sohu.com/a/204516173_160274

https://gs.ctrip.com/html5/you/travels/66/2167136.html

https://www.sohu.com/a/168622936_355964

http://blog.sina.com.cn/s/blog_5f557f640102wzpa.html

http://www.zj.xinhuanet.com/2020-06/06/c_1126081876.htm

https://www.sohu.com/a/238340714_100014198

https://zj.zjol.com.cn/red_boat.html?id=100105882

https://www.meipian.cn/1t0xz4zw

http://www.wenzhougeming.com/newshow.asp?id=401&cla=17,18,

文化活动五：红色文化教育(三)

Cultural Activity (5): Red Culture Education III

文化寻踪之浙里村落 Ancient Towns

➢ 龙泉市住龙镇
Zhulong Town, Longquan City

住龙镇位于钱塘江源头乌溪江上游，地处浙闽两省交界处。这是一座历史悠久、人杰地灵、极具魅力的红色小镇。住龙镇还是龙泉市的重要林业乡镇之一。全镇森林总覆盖率为93.7%，素有“浙西南林海”之称。这里风光秀美，山水相依，有马尾坑瀑布、西井生态沟、披云山革命教育基地、白岩张家大院等。

Zhulong Town is near to the upper reaches of the Wuxi River, the headwaters of the Qiantang River, and at the junction of Zhejiang and Fujian. It is a red town with a long history, outstanding people and great charm. Zhulong Town is also one of the important forestry towns in Longquan, with a total forest coverage rate up to 93.7%, hence the name "Forest Sea in Southwest Zhejiang". The town boasts a beautiful natural scenery, and abundant cultural landscapes, such as Maweikeng Waterfall, Xijing Ecological Ditch, Mountain Piyun Revolutionary Education Base, Baiyan Zhang's Courtyard, etc.

文化寻踪之浙里印记 Cultural Imprints

➢ 红色文化 Red Culture

披云山苏维埃政府旧址 The Former Site of Soviet Government in Mountain Piyun

龙泉市披云山苏维埃政府旧址位于住龙镇住溪村，由龙浦县苏维埃政府旧址、粟裕办公旧址、中共龙浦县委办公旧址、住溪红军街、擂鼓山红军炮台等组成。

The former site of the Soviet government in Mountain Piyun is situated in Zhuxi Village, Zhulong Town, which is composed of the former Soviet government site of Longpu County, the former office of General Su Yu, the former office of the CPC Longpu County Party Committee, Zhuxi Red Army Street, and the Red Army Fort in Mountain Leigu.

文化寻踪之出行贴士 Travel Tips

寻踪之旅载体:红色文化教育(三)

寻踪之旅地点:龙泉市住龙镇

寻踪之旅时间:通常为10月

寻踪信息查询:(1)http://www.longquan.gov.cn/;(2)“掌上龙泉”微信公众平台;(3)搜狐、腾讯等多家网站。

Cultural Activity: Red Culture Education III

Ancient Town: Zhulong Town, Longquan City

Travel Time: Usually in October

For More Information: (1) Please visit http://www.longquan.gov.cn/; (2) Please search on the WeChat public platform "Zhangshang Longquan"; (3) Please visit the websites such as Sohu, Tencent, etc.

参考资料

https://zj.zjol.com.cn/news.html?id=858719

https://www.douban.com/note/725455202/?from=author

https://www.sohu.com/a/415249697_165076

https://u.323000.net/?token=1480992786

http://www.lsnews.com.cn/zt/2019/zhexinan/jyjd/jdjd/201902/t20190228_154201.shtml

https://zj.zjol.com.cn/news/637352.html

11月 November

文化活动一：佛堂『十月十』民俗文化节
Cultural Activity (1): Fotang Folk Cultural Festival on October 10th of the Lunar Calendar

文化活动二：时节
Cultural Activity (2): Harvest Festival

文化活动三：许家山石头文化节
Cultural Activity (3): Xujiashan Stone Cultural Festival

文化活动四：十月十麻糍文化节（老佛节）
Cultural Activity (4): Muachi Cultural Festival on October 10th of the Lunar Calendar

文化活动一：佛堂“十月十”民俗文化节

Cultural Activity (1):

Fotang Folk Cultural Festival on October 10th of the Lunar Calendar

文化寻踪之浙里村落 Ancient Towns

➢ 义乌市佛堂镇

Fotang Town, Yiwu City

佛堂镇位于浙江省义乌市，是中国历史文化名镇。佛堂镇历史悠久，以佛教文化闻名。民国时期佛堂镇因其经济繁荣被誉为浙东四大重镇之一。发达的商埠经济造就了古镇佛堂极其深厚的历史文化底蕴。

Fotang Town, which is located in Yiwu City, Zhejiang Province, is a famous historical and cultural town in China. Fotang town has a long history and is famous for its Buddhism culture. During the period of the Republic of China, Fotang Town was known as one of four important towns in eastern Zhejiang for its prosperous economy. The developed commercial port economy has created a profound historical and cultural heritage of the ancient town Fotang.

文化寻踪之浙里印记 Cultural Imprints

➤ 建筑文化
Architectural Culture

双林寺 Shuanglin Temple

双林寺位于浙江省义乌市佛堂镇罗汉堂，为南朝梁时傅大士所建，是历史上著名的东方佛教活动中心，具有深厚的文化底蕴。双林寺记载着傅大士的神奇传说，拥有云黄寺千年罗汉松、晋朝瓦当、清代石碑。

Located in Luohan Hall, Fotang Town, Yiwu City, Zhejiang Province, Shuanglin Temple was bulit by Great Master Fu (China's Vimalakirti Master and Maitreya incarnation), and was a famous oriental Buddhist activity center in history with profound cultural heritage. Shuanglin Temple records the famous legend of Fu, and boasts a thousand-year-old podocarpus of Yunhuang Temple, the tiles of the Jin Dynasty and a stone tablet of the Qing Dynasty.

➤ 非遗文化
Intangible Cultural Heritage

传统制糖技艺 Traditional Sugar Making Technique

义乌种植甘蔗历史悠久，所产红糖也十分有名。义乌红糖的生产和

制造过程俗称"绞糖"。清朝顺治年间,佛堂人贾维承从福建引进种蔗制糖技术,用传统老式的牛拉木榨糖车的式样和做法制成红糖。

Yiwu has a long history of sugarcane planting, and its produce, brown sugar is also very famous. The production and manufacturing process of Yiwu brown sugar is commonly known as "Jiaotang" (wringing out sugar). During the reign of Emperor Shunzhi (1638–1661) of the Qing Dynasty, Jia Weicheng, a local of Fotang Town, brought in surgarcane planting and sugar making technique, and used cows to to pull wood sugar cart and wring out sugar, enabling the production of sugarcane to become commercially viable.

义乌"抬阁跷" Yiwu Taigeqiao

义乌"抬阁跷"是本地的一种传统祭祀活动,在2008年被列入第三批浙江省非物质文化遗产名录。义乌阁跷每台约1米见方,0.9米高,周围饰有小围栏,特制小平台,台上或站或坐有2至3名童男童女。他们装扮成历史人物,姿态各异,打扮别致,头顶雉鸡毛,手持长枪、宝剑等,下由4名家人亲戚抬着行进。佛堂"抬阁跷"在每年正月十八日举行。

Taigeqiao (the pavilion carrying ritual) in Yiwu is a traditional local folk sacrificial activity, and it was included in the third catalogue of provincial representative intangible cultural heritages of Zhejiang in 2008. Each Yiwu Geqiao is about 1 meter wide and 0.9 meter high, with special designed platforms and surrounded fences. Two to three young boys and girls stand or sit on the platforms, dressing up as historical figures with different postures and unique costumes, wearing pheasant feathers on their heads, holding spears, swords, etc., and they were carried by four family members and relatives. The activity of Taigeqiao is held on the eighteeth day of the first lunar month each year.

文化寻踪之出行贴士 Travel Tips

寻踪之旅载体:佛堂“十月十”民俗文化节

寻踪之旅地点:浙江省义乌市佛堂镇

寻踪之旅时间:通常为11月中旬

寻踪信息查询:(1) http://www.yw.gov.cn;(2)“义乌旅游”微信公众平台;(3)搜狐、腾讯等多家网站。

Cultural Activity: Fotang Folk Cultural Festival on October 10th of the Lunar Calendar

Ancient Town: Fotang Town, Yiwu City, Zhejiang Province

Travel Time: Usually in mid-November

For More Information: (1) Please visit http://www.yw.gov.cn; (2) Please search on the WeChat public platform “Yiwu Lvyou”; (3) Please visit the websites such as Sohu, Tencent, etc.

参考资料

https://baike.baidu.com/item/双林寺/5220324?fr=aladdin

http://www.zjich.cn/xiangmu/xiangmushow.html?id=1747

http://www.zjich.cn/xiangmu/xiangmushow.html?id=1168

http://sjk. zjich. cn/ImageData/loadImageData. page? ViewSize=large&DataOwner=XM_ML_DANGAN_FENGMIAN&DataID=223740

https://www.meipian.cn/xk0pq6k

http://english.jinhua.gov.cn/art/2020/11/26/art_1229181171_58890011.html#

http://www.chinadaily.com.cn/global/2019-08/20/content_37503452.htm

http://yiwuzhejiang.chinadaily.com.cn/2020-01/24/c_340798.htm

https://www.meipian.cn/xlaaips

https://www.sohu.com/a/127065182_178528

https://www.sohu.com/a/301786736_120055805

http://cs.zjol.com.cn/system/2015/02/05/020500573.shtml

http://www.zjdfz.cn/html/2013/msfw_1111/1991.html

文化活动二：时节

Cultural Activity (2):

Harvest Festival

文化寻踪之浙里村落 Ancient Villages

➢ 桐庐县江南镇深澳村
Shen'ao Village, Jiangnan Town, Tonglu County

深澳村位于浙江省桐庐县富春江南岸天子岗北麓，总面积为7.5公顷。深澳村居呈长方形，中有老街，长500余米，宽约3米，卵石铺面，下筑引泉暗渠（俗称“澳”），澳深水冽，因以名村。深澳村的历史非常悠久，有文字记载的始于南宋初期，主要由申屠氏迁居桐溪而形成，距今已有1000多年了。深澳村的传统风俗有时节（丰收节）、水龙会、舞狮、舞龙等。传统手工艺有造坑边纸、绣花、贴画等。深澳村凭借深厚的历史和文化积淀、独特的地理环境和众多的文物古迹，成为国家级历史文化名村。

Shen'ao Village is located in the north of Hill Tianzigang, on the south bank of the Fuchun River, Tonglu County, Zhejiang Province, with a total area of 7.5 hectares. The village is rectangular, and there is an old street with a length of more than 500 meters and a width of about 3 meters. It is paved with pebbles and below is the construction of underdrains (commonly known as "*ao*"), in which the underground water is deep and clear, hence the name of the villiage Shen'ao (meaning deep and clear). The village has a very profound history. According to the written records, it was first established in the Southern Song Dynasty, which was more than a thousand years ago. Shen'ao Village is mainly formed by the relocation of the Shentu family within the region near the Tongxi Stream. The traditional custom of Shen'ao Village include the Harvest Festival, lion dance, and dragon dance, etc. The traditional handicrafts include pit-making paper, embroidery, stickers, etc. With its profound history, cultural accumulation, unique geographical environment, and many cultural relics and historic sites, Shen ' ao Ancient Village has become a national historical and cultural village.

文化寻踪之浙里印记 Cultural Imprints

➢ 建筑文化 Architectural Culture

申屠氏宗祠 Shentu's Ancestral Hall

申屠氏宗祠，始建于清代，坐北朝南，布局为五间三进，通面阔19.5米，通进深45.28米。宗祠以天井为中心，为封闭的组合建筑，采用石木混合的梁架结构。整座宗祠古朴而庄重，犹如一部厚重的家族史书。

First built in the Qing Dynasty, facing south, Shentu's Ancestral Hall has five constructions in three rows, with a width of 19.5 meters and a depth of 45.28 meters. Centered on the patio, the ancestral hall has enclosed composite buildings and adopts the mixed structure of stone and wood beams, etc. The whole ancestral hall is ancient and solemn, which is like a heavy family history book.

➢ 非遗文化
Intangible Cultural Heritage

深澳高空狮子 Shen'ao High-Altitude Lion Dance

高空狮子起源于东汉年间，时逢孙权为母祝寿，当地人为取悦吴帝遂筹备了高空狮子表演。尔后当地举行庙会祭祀或元宵节时，都把高空狮子作为必备节目之一。深澳高空双狮雌雄一对，各长 1.5 米左右，通体金毛，腿部绘有神火，下巴能上下自由开启，其腰身用竹篾圈连接而成，挂有金色彩球。表演时双狮抢球，横杆上下一人拉动彩球，一人拉狮子，一先一后使双狮随彩珠上下同步追彩球，十分精彩。

The high-altitude lion dance originated in the Eastern Han Dynasty. The locals organized a high-altitude lion dance show to appeal to the Emperor Wu when Sun Quan (the founder of the Wu Dynasty that ruled over of the Three Kingdoms) celebrated his mother's birthday. Afterwards, whenever the local temple fair or the Lantern Festival was held, the high-altitude lion dance has been one of the essential shows. Shen'ao high-altitude lion dance requires a pair of female and male lions, each about 1.5 meters long, with golden hair on the whole body, painted with magic fire on the legs, and the chin can be opened up and down freely. Its waist is connected by a bamboo strip ring hanging a golden colored ball. The two lions scramble for the ball. One performer pulls the ball, while the other pulls the lion. Their tacit cooperation makes the two lions chase the colored ball simultaneously, which is very exciting.

文化寻踪之出行贴士 Travel Tips

寻踪之旅载体:时节

寻踪之旅地点:浙江省杭州市桐庐县江南镇深澳村

寻踪之旅时间:通常为11月

寻踪信息查询:(1)http://www.tlnews.com.cn;(2)"桐庐博物馆"微信公众平台;(3)搜狐、腾讯等多家网站。

Cultural Activity: Harvest Festival

Ancient Town: Shen'ao Village, Jiangnan Town, Tonglu County, Hangzhou City, Zhejiang Province

Travel Time: Usually in November

For More Information: (1) Please visit http://www.tlnews.com.cn; (2) Please search on the WeChat public platform "Tonglu Museum"; (3) Please visit the websites such as Sohu, Tencent, etc.

参考资料

http://wwj.zj.gov.cn/art/2019/12/3/art_1228976943_40721426.html

http://www.tcmap.com.cn/zhejiangsheng/tonglu_jiangnanzhen_shenaocun.html

http://www.bytravel.cn/landscape/81/shentushizonghandiejieting.html

https://www.sohu.com/a/217668803_388514
https://www.sohu.com/a/256601481_714583
https://wenku.baidu.com/view/084986f982c4bb4cf7ec4afe04a1b0717ed5b3e3.html
https://xw.qq.com/cmsid/20200131A051DW00
https://mp.weixin.qq.com/s/ApSQaf-kxkcZLGWaeJ6apQ
https://mp.weixin.qq.com/s/jzVURk-juzUaM_9ldMF5Dg
https://hzdaily.hangzhou.com.cn/hzrb/html/2016-11/22/content_2408313.htm
http://www. tlnews. com. cn/xwpd/tlxw/content/2019-04/10/content_8882693.htm

文化活动三：许家山石头文化节

Cultural Activity (3): Xujiashan Stone Cultural Festival

文化寻踪之浙里村落 Ancient Villages

➢ 宁海县茶院乡许家山村

Xujiashan Village, Chayuan Township, Ninghai County

始建于南宋末年的许家山村，位于宁海县茶院乡西南山区。许家山村是宁波市规模最大、保存最完整的石头古村。近6万平方米的核心保护区里，三合院和四合院建筑格局完整，历代先人利用当地丰富的玄武岩资源建设家园。随处可见的石墙、石窗、石路、石桥、石巷、石井、石磨等，令人不得不惊叹先辈的勤劳与智慧。

Xujiashan Village, founded in the late Southern Song Dynasty, is located in the southwest mountainous area of Chayuan Town, Ninghai County. Xujiashan Village is the largest and best-preserved ancient stone village in Ningbo. In the core conservation area of nearly 60,000 square meters, the building layout of the quadrangle dwellings is complete. The ancestors of the past generations used the rich basalt resources in the local area to build their homes. The stone walls, stone windows, stone roads, stone bridges, stone lanes, stone wells, stone mills, etc., can be seen everywhere in the village, which makes people to marvel at the hard work and wisdom of the ancestors.

文化寻踪之浙里印记 Cultural Imprints

➢ 建筑文化 Architectural Culture

石屋建筑群 Stone House Complex

许家山村是浙东沿海山地石屋建筑群落的典范，其原生态的建筑、文化、巷道等，成为原始山村生活的活化石。有"石头王国"之称的许家山村有200余幢石屋。石屋的墙体材料用黑色玄武岩堆垒而成。该村不仅保存着完整的石屋、石院、石墙、石巷、石桥、石路、石凳等组合资源，同时还延续着传统的生活方式，比如用牛耕田、制番薯粉、做番薯烧酒、捣年糕、竹编等。

Xujiashan Village is a model of the stone house building community in the coastal mountainous areas of eastern Zhejiang. The original ecological architecture, culture, roadway of the village have become a living fossil of life in a primitive mountain village. Xujiashan, also known as the "Kingdom of Stones", has more than 200 stone houses. The wall material of the stone house is made of black basalt. The village not only preserves the complete combination of stone houses, stone courtyards, stone walls, stone lanes, stone bridges, stone roads, stone benches, etc., but also keeps the traditional lifestyle, such as cattle farming, making sweet potato flour, making sweet potato spirit, pounding rice cakes, bamboo weaving, etc.

文化寻踪之出行贴士 Travel Tips

寻踪之旅载体：许家山石头文化节

寻踪之旅地点：浙江省宁波市宁海县茶院乡许家山村

寻踪之旅时间：通常为11月

寻踪信息查询：(1)http://nh.cnnb.com.cn/；(2)"许家山石头村"微信公众平台；(3)搜狐、腾讯等多家网站。

Cultural Activity: Xujiashan Stone Cultural Festival

Ancient Village: Xujiashan Village, Chayuan Township, Ninghai County, Ningbo City, Zhejiang Province

Travel Time: Usually in November

For More Information: (1) Please visit http://nh.cnnb.com.cn/; (2) Please search on the WeChat public platform "Xujiashan Shitoucun"; (3) Please visit the websites such as Sohu, Tencent, etc.

参考资料

http://nh.cnnb.com.cn/system/2014/12/01/011099203.shtml

http://nh.cnnb.com.cn/system/2010/12/23/010034506.shtml

https://zjnews.zjol.com.cn/zjnews/zjxw/201810/t20181017_8497503.shtml

http://news.cnnb.com.cn/system/2013/03/12/007655744.shtml

http://blnews.cnnb.com.cn/system/2018/11/27/011934908.shtml

https://www.sohu.com/a/126822900_395073

文化活动四：十月十麻糍文化节（老佛节）

Cultural Activity (4):

Muachi Cultural Festival on October 10th of the Lunar Calendar

文化寻踪之浙里村落 Ancient Villages

➢ 江山市大陈乡大陈村

Dachen Village, Dachen Township, Jiangshan City

大陈村是清末江山至常山的主要驿道，素有“江南古村落”的美称。这个拥有600多年历史、被誉为“十里环山皆松树，天下应无第二园”的地方，旧以经商办学扬名。近年，又以弘扬传统文化与中国村歌发源地闻名遐迩。明朝永乐初徽州汪氏迁入此处，经后人苦心经营，人丁逐渐兴旺，并创建了一个以徽派建筑为主的古村落。古村落的建筑以清代为主，现存古民宅、古祠堂、古戏台等古迹111处，其中汪氏宗祠为杰出代表。

Dachen Village was the main post road from Jiangshan to Changshan in the late Qing Dynasty, and is known as the “Ancient Village in the

South of the Yangtze River". With a history of more than 600 years, this place is reputed as "a village surrounded by the mountains with massive pine trees, and no second village can compare with it". Dachen Village used to be famous for engaging in business and running schools; in recent years, it has got a fame for promoting traditional culture and being the birthplace of Chinese village songs. At the beginning of the reign of Emperor Yongle in the Ming Dynasty, the ancestors, Wang family from Huizhou moved here. Through generations' efforts, the family gradually prospered and built an ancient village featured by Huizhou style architecture, which mostly could be dated back to the Qing Dynasty. Until today, there are 111 historical sites in the village, such as ancient houses, ancient ancestral halls, and ancient stages, etc., among which Wang's Ancestral Hall is one of the most outstanding representatives.

文化寻踪之浙里印记 Cultural Imprints

➢ 建筑文化 Architectural Culture

汪氏宗祠 Wang's Ancestral Hall

大陈古村落有79处清至20世纪初期的徽派建筑。汪氏宗祠是保存相当完好的一座,始建于1866年,一直作为汪氏族人祭祀办学之所。汪氏宗祠布局为三进二天井,白墙、灰瓦、马头墙。门前门楼为三重出跳飞檐,各层以花拱承重。大门两侧檐下各设五对有关人物故事的牛腿,有拿箫、持拐杖、扶羊头等栩栩如生的镂空雕刻。

There are 79 Huizhou style buildings in Dachen Village, which can be dated back to the years from the Qing Dynasty to the early 20th century. Among them, Wang's Ancestral Hall is quite well-preserved. First built in 1866, the hall had always been used as a place for worshipping and schools for Wang's clan. Wang's Ancestral Hall consists of three rows of constructions and two patios, with white walls, gray tiles, and horse-head-shaped walls. The gate tower has triple-floor spiked-up edges, and each floor is supported by the arches. Under the eaves on both sides of the gate, there are five pairs of corbels for character stories, carved with lifelike hollow sculptures, such as holding a flute, holding a cane, and raising a sheep's head, etc.

➢ 非遗文化
Intangible Cultural Heritage

村歌文化 Village Song Culture

大陈村甜美的村歌让人印象深刻。村支书唱着村歌《妈妈的那碗大陈面》一路唱到北京，获得全国村歌十大金曲大奖。首届全国村歌之星演唱大赛就在大陈村举行。近年来，通过村干部领唱，村民代表、党员学唱，群众跟着唱的方式，把村歌唱进了央视、省人民大会堂，还被制作成MV，作为国礼赠给参加G20杭州峰会的外国元首与嘉宾。凭借村歌的魅力，大陈村荣获了“全国村歌示范基地”“中国村歌发祥地”等称号。大陈村歌成了具有鲜明乡愁元素的“金名片”，村歌也成为当地村民唱响幸福生活的最强音。

Dachen Village's village song is impressive. The village's person in charge sang the village song *A Bowl of Dachen Noodle Made by Mum* in Beijing, and won the Top Ten Golden Melody Award in the national village song competition. The first National Village Song Star Singing Competition was held in Dachen. In recent years, village cadres led the singing, village representatives and party members learned to sing, and the masses followed. The village songs were sung on CCTV and the Provincial Great Hall of the People. They were also made into MVs and presented as national gifts to foreign heads of state and guests participating in the G20. Owing to the charm of the village songs, Dachen Village has won honors, such as the "National Village Song Demonstration Base" and "Birthplace of Chinese Village Songs".

江山老佛节 Old Buddha Festival in Jiangshan

十月初十,是著名的大陈"老佛节",又称麻糍节,全村捣麻糍声此起彼伏,香味四处飘逸,家家户户大宴宾朋,整个村庄热闹非凡。该节日已经被列入省非遗名录。江山老佛节分上路乡和下路乡老佛节。其中,下路乡的老佛节以大陈、上余、四都、双塔街道、清湖等地最有特色。虽然上路乡和下路乡的迎佛节的内容、形式有所不同,但都是当地群众的一项文娱活动,是每年秋收后,在农闲季节庆祝丰收、酬谢上天的一项活动,也是当地农民的会亲节。它们的活动经费均由各祠堂拨出一些田租租息,来支付迎佛节请戏班、抬香炉、佛亭、台阁等的费用。

The famous "Old Buddha Festival", also known as the Muachi Cultural Festival, falls on the tenth day of the tenth month of the lunar calendar. On that day, the whole village will be busy with making Muachi, and holding banquets with their friends and relatives. The festival has been included in the provincial intangible cultural heritage list. The Jiangshan Old Buddha Festival is observed mainly in the following two areas, respectively, Shanglu Township and Xialu Township. Although the celebration contents and formats slightly differ in the two areas, both are important recreational activities for the local people. It is an event to celebrate the harvest and reward God during the slack season after the autumn harvest each year; it is also an important occasion to meet the relatives and friends. The funds of the festival are all set aside by the ancestral halls, covering the expenses to invite theatrical troupes, carry the incense burner, the Buddhist pavilion, etc.

红色文化
Red Culture

中国工农红军北上抗日先遣队大陈纪念馆 Dachen Memorial Hall of the Red Army Anti-Japanese Northward Advance Troop

先遣队在江山的战斗情况，在《粟裕战争回忆录》中有明确记载。纪念馆占地面积200余平方米。馆内展厅以图文并茂、实物陈列、视频雕塑的形式，展现了红军挺进浙江、创建革命根据地的光辉历程，再现了党和红军与江山群众患难与共、鱼水相依的深情厚谊。

The fighting situation of the advance troop in Jiangshan was clearly recorded in the *War Memoirs of Su Yu*. The exhibition hall of the war covers an area of more than 200 square meters, and shows the glorious history of the Red Army advancing to Zhejiang and establishing a revolutionary base in the form of pictures and texts, physical displays, and video sculptures, and reproduces the deep friendship between the Party and the Red Army and the people of Jiangshan.

文化寻踪之出行贴士 Travel Tips

寻踪之旅载体:十月十麻糍文化节(老佛节)

寻踪之旅地点:浙江省江山市大陈乡大陈村

寻踪之旅时间:通常为11月

寻踪信息查询:(1)http://www.js-news.cn/;(2)"书香大陈"微信公众平台;(3)搜狐、腾讯等多家网站。

Cultural Activity: Muachi Cultural Festival on October 10th of the Lunar Calendar

Ancient Town: Dachen Village, Dachen Township, Jiangshan City, Zhejiang Province

Travel Time: Usually in November

For More Information: (1) Please visit http://www.js-news.cn/; (2) Please search on the WeChat public platform "Shuxiang Dachen"; (3) Please visit the websites such as Sohu, Tencent, etc.

参考资料

http://www.zjich.cn/xiangmu/xiangmushow.html?id=1173

http://www.21js.com/html/2017/02/267102.shtml

https://baijiahao.baidu.com/s?id=1683976600770069046&wfr=spider&for=pc

http://www.360doc.com/content/20/1029/07/4993693_942951910.shtml

http://jsnews.zjol.com.cn/jsxww/system/2014/09/16/018449723.shtml

https://www.douban.com/note/725756224/

http://www.jiangshan.gov.cn/art/2020/10/15/art_1225864_59016976.html

http://news.qz828.com/system/2014/05/23/010810465.shtml

http://news.qz828.com/system/2014/10/24/010906265.shtml

https://baijiahao.baidu.com/s?id=1652141567849481043&wfr=spider&for=pc

https://zjnews.zjol.com.cn/202104/t20210409_22362988.shtml

https://www.sohu.com/a/272468348_103365

https://www.meipian.cn/1wp8i1id

https://www.sohu.com/a/285114299_171287

https://www.sohu.com/a/363662483_100040492

December 12月

安昌腊月风情节
The Style Festival in the Twelfth Lunar Month of Anchang

安昌腊月风情节

The Style Festival in the Twelfth Lunar Month of Anchang

文化寻踪之浙里村落 Ancient Towns

➤ 绍兴市柯桥区安昌镇

Anchang Town, Keqiao District

安昌镇是中国历史文化名镇，也是一个具有千年历史的典型江南水乡古镇。相传大禹曾在镇东涂山娶妻成家。896年，钱镠奉唐王朝之命屯兵该地平董昌之乱，故名安昌。现今，古镇留存的非遗资源众多，尤以“水乡风情”“师爷故里”“腊月习俗”等令中外游客流连忘返。2008年，绍兴县（现绍兴市柯桥区）被命名为浙江省首批民族传统节日“春节”的保护地，而安昌镇的腊月风情节最令人向往。

Anchang Ancient Town is a famous historical and cultural town, and also a typical ancient water town in the south of the Yangtze River with a thousand-year history. In 896, Qian Liu was ordered by the Tang Dynasty government to garrison the place to suppress Dong Chang's Rebellion, hence the name Anchang. Nowadays, there are many intangible cultural heritage resources remaining in the ancient town, among which the activities such as "water town style", "the hometown of Shiye (the private adviser)", and "the twelfth lunar month custom" have attracted greatly Chinese and foreign tourists. In 2008, Shaoxing County (now Keqiao District, Shaoxing City) was named as the protected area of the spring festival, the first batch of ethnic traditional festivals in Zhejiang, and the "Style Festival in Twelfth Lunar Month of Anchang" is the most desirable.

文化寻踪之浙里印记 Cultural Imprints

➢ 非遗文化 Intangible Cultural Heritage

绍兴宣卷 Shaoxing Xuanjuan

绍兴宣卷是浙江绍兴地区的"五大曲种"之一，它形成于清代后期，清末民初流传上海、杭州、苏州、宁波等地，至今已有一百五十多年的历史。绍兴宣卷是一种具有宗教色彩的说唱艺术，主要用于祀神祈福活动。宣卷的唱本，即卷本，通称"宝卷"。艺人在演唱时，置卷本于桌，照本宣唱，故称宣卷。绍兴宣卷的卷本，总数百本左右。宣卷的内容，有的与佛教经籍有关，有的与戏曲同目。

Shaoxing Xuanjuan is one of the five most influential operas in Shaoxing, Zhejiang. It was formed in the late Qing Dynasty and spread to Shanghai, Hangzhou, Suzhou, Ningbo and other areas in the late Qing

Dynasty and the early Republic of China, with a history of more than 150 years. Shaoxing Xuanjuan is a religious art form combing talking and singing, mainly used for worshiping gods and praying for blessings. The opera libretto is commonly called as "baojuan". When the artist sings, one puts the opera libretto on the table and sings accordingly, hence the name Xuanjuan. There are about one hundred volumes of Shaoxing Xuanjuan librettos. Some are related to Buddhist scriptures, and some are the same as traditional operas.

水乡社戏 Village Opera in the Water Town

水乡社戏是浙江农村和城镇一种以戏剧表演为核心的民俗活动,它具有祭神和娱人相结合的特点,普遍流行于绍兴地区。绍兴的社戏大致分为年规戏、庙会戏、平安戏、偿愿戏等类型,其中以庙会戏为主。社戏的演出程式比较固定,社戏的舞台可分成庙台、祠堂台、河台(水台)、街台、草台等,其中以河台(水台)最具特色,被称作"水乡舞台"。这是一种极具水乡特色的伸出式舞台,后台在岸上,前台在水中,为观众创造了一种水上、岸上同时观看演出的条件。水乡社戏扎根民间,深受广大观众喜爱,至今仍可在绍兴地区见到它的踪影。

The village opera is a kind of folklore activity centered on drama performance in rural areas and towns of Zhejiang. The opera has the characteristics of combining scarifice to gods and entertainment, and it is popular in Shaoxing. The village opera in Shaoxing can be roughly categorized as the annual opera, the temple fair opera, the opera blessing for peace, and the opera for redeeming a wish, among which the temple fair opera is the dominance. The performance program of the village opera is relatively fixed, and the locations of stages can be in a temple, ancestral hall, riverbank (water stage), street and the temporarily built one, etc. Among them, the riverbank stage is the most distinctive and is called the "water town stage". This is a kind of outstretched stage with the characteristics of a water town. With the backstage on the shore and the performance stage built on the river, the show enables audience to watch on a boat and on the shore. The village opera takes root in the folk and is deeply loved by the audience. Nowadays, such kind of performances can still be seen in Shaoxing.

绍兴师爷故事 The Stories of Shaoxing Private Advisers

古人云:"天下师爷出绍兴,绍兴师爷出安昌。"安昌师爷人才辈出,明清时期,外出做师爷者不下万余人,晚清更是安昌师爷的鼎盛期。绍兴师爷故事是由一系列以"绍兴师爷"为主要人物的轶事趣闻组成的民间故事,以及文人据此加工创作的机智故事。其内容丰富,地方特色鲜明,题材广泛,情节跌宕,充满神奇和智慧。绍兴师爷故事的原创性和地域性是绍兴文化遗产的重要组成部分。

As the old adage goes, "Private advisers of China mainly came from Shaoxing, while private advisers of Shaoxing mainly came from Anchang." Anchang boasted a large number of talents who served as private advisers. During the Ming and Qing Dynasties, there were more than 10,000 people who served as private advisers, and the late Qing Dynasty was the heyday of Anchang private advisers. The stories of Shaoxing private advisers are a series of folktales composed of anecdotes and witty stories created by literati, featuring rich content and distinctive local characteristics. The stories have a wide range of subjects full of magic and wisdom, ups and downs. The originality and regionality of the stories is an important part of Shaoxing's cultural heritage.

绍兴酱油酿造技艺 Shaoxing Traditional Soy Sauce Making Skills

绍兴是中国酱文化的重要代表地,"无绍不成酱"是对绍兴酱产业、酱文化的概括。绍兴的制酱业起于民间。20世纪初期,绍兴的酱园作坊多达500家,当时就有"绍酒行天下,酱园遍全国"的风采。安昌仁昌酱园创建于清光绪年间,已有100多年的历史,其酱油传统酿造技艺在2009年被列入省非物质文化遗产名录。

Shaoxing is an important representative place of Chinese sauce culture. "No sauce can be made without Shaoxing" is a generalization of the sauce industry and sauce culture of Shaoxing. Shaoxing's sauce industry started from the folks. In the early days of the Republic of China, there were as many as five hundred sauce workshops in Shaoxing, therefore it was reputed as "Shaoxing wine sold all over China, while Shaoxing sauce workshops set up all over the country". Renchang Workshop was founded in the Guangxu period of the Qing Dynasty and has a history of over 100 years. Its traditional soy sauce making skills were included in the provincial intangible cultural heritage list in 2009.

文化寻踪之出行贴士 Travel Tips

寻踪之旅载体:安昌腊月风情节

寻踪之旅地点:浙江省绍兴市柯桥区安昌镇

寻踪之旅时间:通常为12月或1月

寻踪信息查询:(1)http://www.kq.gov.cn;(2)"古镇安昌"微信公众平台;(3)搜狐、腾讯等多家网站。

Cultural Activity: The Style Festival in the Twelfth Lunar Month of Anchang

Ancient Town: Anchang Town, Keqiao District, Shaoxing City, Zhejiang Province

Travel Time: Usually in December or January

For More Information: (1) Please visit http://www.kq.gov.cn; (2) Please search on the WeChat public platform "Guzhen Anchang"; (3) Please visit the websites such as Sohu, Tencent, etc.

参考资料

http://www.ihchina.cn/Article/Index/detail?id=15241

http://www.360doc.com/content/19/0611/14/64597709_841750245.shtml

http://www.ihchina.cn/Article/Index/detail?id=21111

http://www.ihchina.cn/Article/Index/detail?id=13723

http://www.zjich.cn/xiangmu/xiangmushow.html?id=299

https://www.sohu.com/a/258521808_740471

http://www.zjich.cn/xiangmu/xiangmushow.html?id=607

https://www.sohu.com/a/400134939_663865

http://www.zjich.cn/xiangmu/xiangmushow.html?id=1073

http://www.chinadaily.com.cn/opinion/2014-09/12/content_18588756.htm

编号	推荐活动		浙里村落	浙里印记	所在城市
1	1月	鱼文化节	南浔区和孚镇获港村	**建筑文化** 南苕胜境 演教禅寺 **名人文化** 章荣初 章鸿钊 **非遗文化** 荻港民间丝竹 **农业文化** 湖州桑基鱼塘系统	湖州
2	2月	正月十四元宵行会	宁海县前童镇	**非遗文化** 正月十四元宵行会 十里红妆 **建筑文化** 八卦水系	宁波
3		元宵节	嵊州市崇仁镇	**建筑文化** 崇仁古建筑群 玉山公祠 **非遗文化** 大头荷 越剧	绍兴
4		“台阁”年俗文化节	诸暨市枫桥镇	**名人文化** 王冕故地 枫桥三贤 **非遗文化** 台阁	绍兴
5		观海卫都神行会	慈溪市观海卫镇鸣鹤古镇	**建筑文化** 金仙寺 24间走马楼 银号 **非遗文化** 观海卫都神行会 宁波走书 越窑青瓷烧制技艺 **红色文化** 宓大昌大屋	宁波

续表

编号	推荐活动		浙里村落	浙里印记	所在城市
6	2月	武义抬阁	武义县俞源乡俞源村	**建筑文化** 俞氏宗祠 声远堂 裕后堂 **非遗文化** 武义抬阁 武义泥水画	金华
7	3月	浙江油菜花节	仙居县皤滩镇	**建筑文化** 皤滩古建筑群落 **非遗文化** 仙居花灯 石窗艺术	台州
8			仙居县高迁村	**建筑文化** 省身堂 慎德堂 **非遗文化** 卵石镶嵌技艺	台州
9		河阳非遗文化节	缙云县新建镇河阳村	**建筑文化** 八士门街 廉让之间 箬樵路 **非遗文化** 缙云剪纸	丽水
10	4月	畲族三月三节	景宁畲族自治县鹤溪镇	**建筑文化** 景宁孔庙 **非遗文化** 畲族民歌 畲族婚俗 景宁畲族祭祀仪式 畲族三月三	丽水
11		乌镇香市	桐乡市乌镇	**非遗文化** 乌镇竹编 乌镇香市 乌镇水阁 乌镇蚕桑习俗 蓝印花布印染技艺	嘉兴

续表

编号	推荐活动		浙里村落	浙里印记	所在城市
12	4月	三月三，踏沙滩 三月二十三开洋节	象山县石浦镇	**非遗文化** 开洋节/谢洋节 象山渔民号子	宁波
13		蚕花庙会	德清县新市镇	**建筑文化** 新市河埠群 南圣堂 刘王庙戏台题记 **非遗文化** 新市蚕花庙会	湖州
14		龙游县的清明祭祖灯会	龙游县石佛乡三门源村	**建筑文化** 叶氏建筑群（艺术砖雕） **非遗文化** 龙游皮纸制作技艺 龙游婺剧 龙游发糕制作	衢州
15		三月三祭祖典礼	建德市大慈岩镇新叶村	**建筑文化** 新叶祠堂 抟云塔建筑群 **非遗文化** 新叶昆曲 新叶三月三	杭州
16	5月	护国随粮王信俗会	嘉善县西塘镇	**建筑文化** 西塘古民居 **非遗文化** 传统纽扣制作技艺 八珍糕制作技艺 京砖烧制技艺 嘉善宣卷 嘉善田歌 护国随粮王信俗会	嘉兴
17		江山旅游	江山市廿八都镇	**非遗文化** 廿八都木偶戏 廿八都山歌	衢州

续表

编号	推荐活动		浙里村落	浙里印记	所在城市
18	6月	品慈城杨梅	江北区慈城镇	**建筑文化** 慈城古建筑群 **非遗文化** 水磨年糕手工制作技艺 骨木镶嵌技艺	宁波
19		杨梅节	松阳县西屏镇	**建筑文化** 延庆寺塔 **非遗文化** 松阳高腔 松阳端午茶	丽水
20	7月	岱山东沙镇弄堂节	岱山县东沙镇	**非遗文化** 舟山渔民号子 舟山锣鼓 岱山布袋木偶戏 祭海	舟山
21		古村文化旅游节（永兴庙会）	绍兴市稽东镇冢斜村	**建筑文化** 永兴公祠 余氏宗祠 余氏老台门 高新屋台门 **名人文化** 状元余煌 河南布政司余炳焘	绍兴
22	8月	黄酒节	越城区东浦镇	**建筑文化** 鲁东村泗龙桥 热诚学堂 **非遗文化** 绍兴黄酒酿制技艺 **名人文化** 徐锡麟	绍兴
23		避暑胜地	武义县武阳镇郭洞村	**建筑文化** 何氏宗祠 新屋里 熟溪桥	金华
24			婺城区汤溪镇寺平村	**建筑文化** 砖雕民居	金华

续表

<table>
<tr><th>编号</th><th colspan="2">推荐活动</th><th>浙里村落</th><th>浙里印记</th><th>所在城市</th></tr>
<tr><td>25</td><td rowspan="4">9月</td><td>九月初一庙会</td><td>富阳区龙门镇</td><td>建筑文化
龙门古建筑群
非遗文化
龙门九月初一庙会</td><td>杭州</td></tr>
<tr><td>26</td><td>观潮节</td><td>海宁市盐官镇</td><td>建筑文化
鱼鳞石塘（钱塘江海塘）
宰相府第风情街
海神庙
安国寺经幢
非遗文化
海宁皮影戏
海宁观潮
名人文化
王国维故居</td><td>嘉兴</td></tr>
<tr><td>27</td><td rowspan="2">菱文化节</td><td>南浔区菱湖镇</td><td>建筑文化
菱湖安澜桥
非遗文化
震远同茶食“三珍”制作技艺
射中村与后羿神话
名人文化
竹墩“三沈”</td><td>湖州</td></tr>
<tr><td>28</td><td>南浔区双林镇</td><td>建筑文化
双林三桥
幻溇古桥群
非遗文化
双林绫绢织造技艺
湖剧
船拳</td><td>湖州</td></tr>
<tr><td>29</td><td rowspan="2">9月</td><td>庆元菇神庙会</td><td>庆元县松源镇大济村</td><td>建筑文化
明清古民居群
名人文化
扁鹊卢医庙</td><td>丽水</td></tr>
<tr><td>30</td><td>赏桂花和红枫等特色树木</td><td>乐清市仙溪镇南阁村</td><td>建筑文化
南阁牌楼群
名人文化
章纶故居</td><td>温州</td></tr>
</table>

续表

编号	推荐活动		浙里村落	浙里印记	所在城市
31	10月	马仙出巡	平阳县顺溪镇	**建筑文化** 顺溪陈氏古民居群 百僧堂 **非遗文化** 平阳木偶戏 马仙信俗 平阳太平钿剪纸 平阳吹打	温州
32		民俗文化节	金华市前仓镇厚吴村	**建筑文化** 吴氏宗祠 **非遗文化** 永康“打罗汉” 婺剧	金华
33		红色文化教育	永嘉县岩坦镇屿北村	**建筑文化** 尚书祠 **非遗文化** 永嘉乱弹 **红色文化** 中共瓯北中心县委旧址钟寿堂	温州
34			永嘉县岩头镇	**建筑文化** 芙蓉村古建筑群 金昭牌坊 **非遗文化** 永嘉花鼓 **红色文化** 红十三军旧址	温州
35			龙泉市住龙镇	**红色文化** 披云山苏维埃政府旧址	丽水
36	11月	佛堂“十月十”民俗文化节	义乌市佛堂镇	**建筑文化** 双林寺 **非遗文化** 传统制糖技艺 义乌“抬阁跷”	金华

续表

编号	推荐活动		浙里村落	浙里印记	所在城市
37	11月	时节	桐庐县江南镇深澳村	**建筑文化** 申屠氏宗祠 **非遗文化** 深澳高空狮子	杭州
38		许家山石头文化节	宁海县茶院乡许家山村	**建筑文化** 石屋建筑群	宁波
39		十月十麻糍文化节（老佛节）	江山市大陈乡大陈村	**建筑文化** 汪氏宗祠 **非遗文化** 村歌文化 江山老佛节 **红色文化** 中国工农红军北上抗日先遣队大陈纪念馆	衢州
40	12月	安昌腊月风情节	绍兴市柯桥区安昌镇	**非遗文化** 绍兴宣卷 水乡社戏 绍兴师爷故事 绍兴酱油酿造技艺	绍兴

图书在版编目(CIP)数据

寻找浙里的乡愁印记:浙江古村落文化寻踪 / 王慧盛编著.
—杭州:浙江工商大学出版社,2021.6
ISBN 978-7-5178-4510-2

Ⅰ.①寻… Ⅱ.①王… Ⅲ.①村落文化—文化研究—浙江 Ⅳ.①K928.5

中国版本图书馆 CIP 数据核字(2021)第104336号

寻找浙里的乡愁印记——浙江古村落文化寻踪
XUNZHAO ZHE LI DE XIANGCHOU YINJI——ZHEJIANG GU CUNLUO WENHUA XUNZONG

王慧盛 编著

责任编辑 张莉娅
责任校对 李远东
封面设计 红羽文化
责任印制 包建辉
出版发行 浙江工商大学出版社
(杭州市教工路198号 邮政编码310012)
(E-mail:zjgsupress@163.com)
(网址:http://www.zjgsupress.com)
电话:0571-88904980,88831806(传真)
排　　版 杭州朝曦图文设计有限公司
印　　刷 杭州高腾印务有限公司
开　　本 710mm×1000mm 1/16
印　　张 18.75　　**印　　量** 2000册
字　　数 281千
版 印 次 2021年6月第1版 2021年6月第1次印刷
书　　号 ISBN 978-7-5178-4510-2
定　　价 65.00元

版权所有 侵权必究

如发现印装质量问题,影响阅读,请和营销与发行中心联系调换
联系电话 0571-88904970